Editor-in-Chief and Founder:
  Lyndon H. LaRouche, Jr.
Editorial Board: *Lyndon H. LaRouche, Jr. , Helga Zepp-LaRouche, Robert Ingraham, Tony Papert, Gerald Rose, Dennis Small, Jeffrey Steinberg, William Wertz*
Co-Editors: *Robert Ingraham, Tony Papert*
Managing Editor: *Nancy Spannaus*
Technology: *Marsha Freeman*
Books: *Katherine Notley*
Ebooks: *Richard Burden*
Graphics: *Alan Yue*
Photos: *Stuart Lewis*
Circulation Manager: *Stanley Ezrol*

INTELLIGENCE DIRECTORS
Counterintelligence: *Jeffrey Steinberg, Michele Steinberg*
Economics: *John Hoefle, Marcia Merry Baker, Paul Gallagher*
History: *Anton Chaitkin*
Ibero-America: *Dennis Small*
Russia and Eastern Europe: *Rachel Douglas*
United States: *Debra Freeman*

INTERNATIONAL BUREAUS
Bogotá: *Miriam Redondo*
Berlin: *Rainer Apel*
Copenhagen: *Tom Gillesberg*
Houston: *Harley Schlanger*
Lima: *Sara Madueño*
Melbourne: *Robert Barwick*
Mexico City: *Gerardo Castilleja Chávez*
New Delhi: *Ramtanu Maitra*
Paris: *Christine Bierre*
Stockholm: *Ulf Sandmark*
United Nations, N.Y.C.: *Leni Rubinstein*
Washington, D.C.: *William Jones*
Wiesbaden: *Göran Haglund*

ON THE WEB
e-mail: eirns@larouchepub.com
www.larouchepub.com
www.executiveintelligencereview.com
www.larouchepub.com/eiw
Webmaster: *John Sigerson*
Assistant Webmaster: *George Hollis*
Editor, Arabic-language edition: *Hussein Askary*

EIR (ISSN 0273-6314) *is published weekly (50 issues), by EIR News Service, Inc.,* P.O. Box 17390, Washington, D.C. 20041-0390. (703) 297-8434

European Headquarters: E.I.R. GmbH, Postfach Bahnstrasse 9a, D-65205, Wiesbaden, Germany Tel: 49-611-73650
Homepage: http://www.eir.de
e-mail: info@eir.de
Director: Georg Neudecker

Montreal, Canada: 514-461-1557
eir@eircanada.ca

Denmark: EIR - Denmark, Sankt Knuds Vej 11, basement left, DK-1903 Frederiksberg, Denmark. Tel.: +45 35 43 60 40, Fax: +45 35 43 87 57. e-mail: eirdk@hotmail.com.

Mexico City: EIR, Sor Juana Inés de la Cruz 242-2 Col. Agricultura C.P. 11360 Delegación M. Hidalgo, México D.F. Tel. (5525) 5318-2301
eirmexico@gmail.com

I0407901

LaRouche Calls for Immediate Trump-Putin Summit To Stop the British Drive for World War III

EDITORIAL

STOP THE BRITISH DRIVE FOR WORLD WAR III

The Bitch Set Him Up!

April 9—Lyndon LaRouche today warned that there is a British-run *coup d'état* in process against the Trump Administration in the United States, which threatens to parlay the stupid and dangerous April 6 air strike against Syria, into a full-fledged thermonuclear confrontation with Russia and China.

It's the British bastards who duped President Trump into attacking Syria, with their lies and false intelligence, LaRouche charged. We have to destroy the British system and all their interests in the United States, he stated. We have to rally the United States to get back on the trajectory that Trump had begun to chart for the country, of cooperation with Russia and China around American System economic policies, including a return to FDR's 1933 Glass-Steagall principle.

Trump and Putin should immediately hold a summit meeting to address the crisis, LaRouche said, and thereby short-circuit the whole British operation. LaRouche strongly endorsed the comments this weekend by veteran German statesman Willy Wimmer, former Secretary of State of the German Defense Ministry, who warned that "people are afraid of a global war, a Third World War," and argued that "the current dramatic situation offers an opportunity for the Russian and U.S. heads of state to meet as soon as possible."

There can be no doubt that the British are behind last week's shocking about-face of Trump's policy. Top British officials are crowing openly over their achievement to date. For example, British Defense Secretary Michael Fallon published an op-ed in the April 9 *Sunday Times* of London, bragging that "the British and American governments have been in close contact at all levels before and after the strikes. ... U.S. Defense Secretary Jim Mattis called me to share their assessment of the regime's culpability. Together we reviewed the options they were considering."

On April 8, British Foreign Secretary Boris Johnson had also claimed that he was coordinating everything with his American counterpart, Secretary of State Rex Tillerson, including Johnson's theatrical cancellation of his scheduled trip to Moscow. "I discussed these plans in detail with Secretary Tillerson," Johnson boasted. "He will visit Moscow as planned and, following the G7 meeting [in Lucca, Italy on April 10-April 11], will be able to deliver that clear and coordinated message to the Russians."

Today's *Sunday Times* elaborated, in an article accompanying the Fallon op-ed, as to what that message would be: "Britain and America will this week directly accuse Russia of complicity in war crimes in Syria and demand that Vladimir Putin pull the rug from Bashar al-Assad's blood-soaked regime." Fallon further wrote: "By proxy, Russia is responsible for every civilian death last week," adding that Putin must now get with the program, by agreeing to the overthrow of the Assad government.

The chances of Putin going along with this British demand, are zero. The chances of the situation spiraling into a thermonuclear confrontation—either in the Middle East or around the Korean Peninsula—are significantly greater than zero, so long as the British are calling the shots.

Having induced Trump to attack Syria based upon their lies, the British are now also orchestrating a storm of opposition to President Trump in the Obama wing of the Democratic Party, calling for Trump's impeachment because of the Syria caper. Trump's actions this week have also weakened him politically among his own base of supporters, both in the United States and internationally, who are shocked and dismayed at what he did—which adds grist to the British mill.

The current situation is extremely dangerous, LaRouche emphasized, and can lead to war in the short term. And it is being brought about entirely by the British, and nothing else. We have to destroy that British imperial system. The citizens of the United States must rally themselves against this British coup. No intelligent person will accept what the British are up to. The only people inside the United States who will back the British, LaRouche said, are brain-drained people who are traitors to the United States.

We have to come down like a hammer on this, in order to stop the British coup to take over the Trump Administration, and the related drive to war. The Schiller Institute's two-day conference this coming April 13-April 14 in New York City, on "U.S.-China Cooperation on the Belt and Road Initiative and Corresponding Ideas in Chinese and Western Philosophy," will present the policy alternative which is capable of destroying the British Empire, permanently.

EIR Contents

www.larouchepub.com Volume 44, Number 15, April 14, 2017

Cover This Week

Control center of the North American Aerospace Defense Command (NORAD).

creative commons

I. The New Economy

NYU TANDON SCHOOL OF ENGINEERING HOSTS

'The New Silk Road: A Global Engineering Renaissance'

by Jason Ross

Brooklyn, April 7—It is imperative that a major shift in U.S. policy be effected, towards economic development centered around implementing improved technologies of infrastructure and manufacturing, and away from British-directed regime change wars and geopolitics. An event held today at the NYU Tandon School of Engineering, cosponsored by the Schiller Institute, provided a significant boost towards making that policy shift. The five-hour conference brought together over 70 engineers and engineering students, businessmen, bankers, and political layers.

The presentations ran the gamut of major infrastructure and development programs worldwide.
The New Silk Road/One Belt, One Road program of China.
The LaRouche approach to understanding the economic value of infrastructure.
The Kra Canal and the Bering Strait crossing;
The long-term sustainability of cross-national infrastructure;
The infrastructure needs of Africa and those of the Americas, such as:
    Closing the Darien Gap,
    Building the Nicaragua Canal,
    Addressing the trillions of dollars of infrastructure deficit in the United States.

The quality of discussion reflected the qualified audience, with questions and discussion on the topics of specific engineering aspects, financing needs, geopolitics and the other reasons more projects are *not* underway, on the security needs for development corridors, and on the political dimensions of getting Trump on-board, and how to ensure that all parties to international projects are able to reap their proper benefits.

The coffee break and post-conference period were abuzz with intense engagement and interest in learning more and on finding other avenues of cooperation and discussion. The major Schiller Institute conference on April 13-April 14 is the perfect follow-up for all participants, and it is hoped that that conference will strike a major blow towards economic cooperation and development, here in the nation's intellectual capital, New York.

The program for the event follows, and video of the presentations and discussion sessions will be posted on the Schiller Institute's *New Paradigm for Mankind* site in short order.

courtesy of Jason Ross

Howard Chang, at the podium during 'The New Silk Road: A Global Engineering Renaissance' conference. Hal Cooper is seated on the left, and Jason Ross is seated on the right.

Program

12:30 Greetings and welcome
Tom Wysmuller, former president, NYU Alumni Association

12:40 The Silk Roads, Old and New: Great Infrastructure for the Future
Howard Chang, PhD, PE, Professor Emeritus of Civil and Environmental Engineering at San Diego State University

1:15 The Economic Value of Infrastructure
Jason Ross, Schiller Institute, co-author, The New Silk Road Becomes the World Land-Bridge

1:45 Changing the World with the Kra Canal
Pakdee Tanapura, International Director of the International Executive Committee for the Study of the Kra Canal Project

2:00 Discussion, audience Q&A

2:30 *Coffee break/networking:* Light refreshments courtesy of the NYU Alumni Association

3:00 Greetings from the Civil Engineering Department

3:05 Infrastructure Needs of the Americas
Albert Pozotrigo, PE, Executive Vice President and Director of Construction Management at M&J Engineering

3:35 Sustainability Needs of the New Silk Road Infrastructure
Richard Trifan, Vice President, The Eurasia Center

4:00 Connecting the Bering Strait: Joining the Americas to the Belt and Road Initiative
Hal Cooper, PhD, PE, Chairman, Seattle Freight Transport Advisory Board

4:30 Roundtable discussion and Q&A
Audience dialogue, discussion of career opportunities

5:20 Concluding remarks and announcements/future events

Speakers

Howard Chang, PhD, PE, Professor Emeritus of Civil and Environmental Engineering at San Diego State University. Dr. Chang has provided professional consulting since 1967, has performed extensive research in the area of water resources engineering, has published over 100 refereed papers in journals and conference proceedings, and is the author of several computer models for channel design and river hydraulics as well as the book *Fluvial Processes in River Engineering*, published by John Wiley & Sons.

Hal Cooper, PhD, PE, Chairman, Freight Transport Advisory Board, Seattle, Washington. Dr. Cooper is a specialist in railroad transportation, with an emphasis on coal transport and intermodal freight. His work on commuter light rail, freight rail, and high-speed rail has included energy requirement analyses for electrified rail. The author of over 150 articles, Dr. Cooper has spoken internationally on proposals for rail across the American continents, including a rail connection across the Bering Strait.

Albert Pozotrigo, PE, Executive Vice President and Director of Construction Management at M&J Engineering. Mr. Pozotrigo is a highly respected chief construction manager who has served on some of the largest NYSDOT projects in New York City, totalling over $650 million, including the Alexander Hamilton Bridge Rehabilitation Project, the reconstruction of FDR Drive, and work on Route 9A. He is the immediate past president of the ASCE Metropolitan Section, and a member of the advisory committee for New York City Technical College.

Jason Ross, Schiller Institute, editor-in-chief of 21st Century Science & Technology. Mr. Ross's work focuses on the intersection between science, infrastructure, and economics, studying the non-scalar and non-local economic value of scientific discovery and infrastructure platforms. He is a co-author of the in-depth report The New Silk Road Becomes the World Land-Bridge and an activist engaged in orienting U.S. economic policy towards long-term investments in science and infrastructure.

Pakdee Tanapura, International Director and Acting Spokesman of the Board of Directors of the International Executive Committee for the Study of the Kra Canal Project in Bangkok, Thailand. Mr. Tanapura has been working on the Kra Canal project across Thailand for over 30 years, organizing conferences that included such participants as the Thai Minister of Transport and Communications, the Global Infrastructure Fund of Japan, advisors to the governments of Indonesia and Malaysia, and American scientists and engineers.

Richard Trifan, V.P. of Government Relations & Trade at The Eurasia Center, and Enterprise Asset Management Business Lead for the New York MTA. Certified in PMP, Prince2 and ITIL to lead global transformation initiatives, specifically where complex assets require sustainability for a lifespan of more than 50 years. Mr. Trifan is a frequent international speaker on the subject of the New Silk Road, and holds memberships with CLM (Council of Logistics Management), APICS (American Production and Inventory Control Society), and the Institute of Asset Management (IAM), and is a Greenbelt in the Six Sigma and 5S disciplines.

Krafft Ehricke: Creating a Knowledge of the Future

The following is an edited version of a speech delivered by Megan Beets to an event held in Houston, Texas on March 25, 2017 to celebrate the 100th anniversary of the birth of Krafft Ehricke.

Megan Beets: Thank you very much for having me today; I'm very excited to speak to you even if for a short time. I'd like to begin by reading something that Krafft Ehricke wrote in 1948. Think about 1948: that was just after the end of World War II; Krafft Ehricke had been in the United States for two years, and he was just beginning to master English. It would be nine more years before the first satellite, Sputnik, would be launched into orbit.

What I'm going to read you is the opening of something he wrote called "Expedition Ares."[1] Written in 1948, this is an imaginary account of space travel in the year 2050, as seen by people *looking back* from the year 2400.

NASA, ESA, and The Hubble Heritage Team

Photograph of Mars taken by the Hubble Space Telescope.

We live in the age of fast-flying, far-reaching space ships, and are proud of what human ingenuity has achieved in this field. Research is going on with ultra-fast ships, reaching half the velocity of light and designed as powerful instruments for visiting our neighboring stars.

But the adult soon forgets the first stumbling steps of childhood, and the first attempts to reach

---

1. "Expedition Ares: A Saga From the Dawn of Interplanetary Travel," *21st Century Science & Technology*, June 2003.

our nearest cosmic vicinity has almost completely vanished from our memory.

Looking back through the centuries, we perceive a chain of heroic deeds which mark Man's grasp at other planets. Only fifty years ago, Glenn Wolf's party landed on Pluto. Their flash light photographs showing the men wading through helium pools amidst fantastic structures of frozen gas which tower into the eternal night, belong to the standard equipment of astronomical books today.

A hundred years ago, Ted Aitken, the most fearless space explorer of his time, died in a bold attempt to reach Saturn. His ship, the famous "Nightmare," was smashed between the rocks of Saturn's rings after a meteor had blown away the navigation room.

A hundred years before his time, Gordon Rockwell opened the golden age of discoveries. He was the first to jump, in his ion-powered "Blizzard," over the great gulf—the vast gap behind Mars, as they called it—and intrude into the dangerous realm of Jupiter's satellites. This pioneer discovered fossils of a strange life on Satellite 111. It blossomed millions of years ago when the giant planet was still the hot, animating center of its extensive system. Rockwell actually founded the cosmic branch of palaeobiologic sciences and made Jupiter's moons an El Dorado of cosmic life research.

Even farther back, old documents reveal the

tragedies connected with the exploration of Venus and tell a tale of Duke Hatchword's "sunny" trip to Mercury... yes, planet after planet unveiled their secrets before the eager spirit and ironclad will of keen explorers.

Yet, there is one planet which must be mentioned separately. Mars, the most familiar outer world for our generation, is connected with the very first beginnings of space travel.

Back in the 20th Century, when tiny rockets climbed a meager two hundred miles (did you ever hear of a "V-2" or a "Neptune 8"?), Mars was the dream goal of those who believed in space travel, actually a fantastic conception when one considers the troubled and primitive world into which they were born. Mars was considered the most interesting planet in the system, the only one that might bear life. Some even dreamed of a Martian civilization, superior to ours, with which a cosmic exchange of ideas might be brought about. Small wonder that Mars became the first planet ever explored by Man.

Circling Earth in small scout rockets, scientists and engineers, dreamers and adventurers, found themselves on the brink of a vast emptiness, beyond which new worlds lured and stimulated their desire to remove the barriers erected between Man and star.

The first attempt to realize these dreams is known in history as "Expedition Ares."

Imagining the Past from the Future

After the introduction, Krafft goes on to depict this first attempted mission to land on Mars. What an incredible and *important* imagination he had! I want to ask you, all of you, today, sitting in this room, to take a moment and think from our standpoint now, in 2017—imagine what mankind in one hundred years might be like. Now imagine, not what *we* will perceive mankind one hundred years from now to be like, but imagine what people in five hundred years will see as they look back on those people, and what will they think of them? How will they perceive their actions?

Now, when you think of these people one hundred years from now, can you imagine a humanity for whom war is something which is unknown? In other words, war is something which children of that time learn about in history books, when they study a more primitive age of Man, but is not something which exists in

civilization. I want you to imagine how *those* people will look back on 2017: what will be the meaning of China's One Belt, One Road to them? Maybe, when these people look back on 2017, they will recall that this was the first year that humanity *finally* began to integrate itself across the entire planet with the World Land-Bridge, and began to become a modern civilization.

Perhaps they'll look back on 2017 and see a population which *finally* took the steps to shut down a ridiculous Wall Street economic system, put Wall Street out of existence, and shut down this gambling and looting system—and replace it with the American System.

And maybe they'll look back on 2017 as the very beginning of actions that were taken which eliminated poverty, for good; which eliminated famine, such that it was no longer known among mankind.

Now, I want you to think about us from their standpoint. Look back at them. Perhaps the year 2117 will be the first year that mankind begins to settle Titan, one of the moons of Saturn. Or, perhaps, we will be far beyond Titan by that point. Perhaps we'll be exploring some of the middle to outer regions of the Solar System.

That play in your imagination, that possibility, should be everyone's understanding of what we today could cause the meaning of the Trump administration to be. I think that the Trump administration may be more aware of this possibility than some have thought, but no matter how aware they are, or not, it doesn't really matter. *We* have to think about our own responsibility for realizing the great potential that I asked you to play with in your imagination. The way that we do that, the way that we understand our task today, to determine the meaning of the Trump administration, is to begin by passing LaRouche's Four Laws To Save the U.S.A. This will allow us to reestablish the American System, first by putting Glass-Steagall in place, to put Wall Street out of its misery; and to put the measures in place to enable the activity that LaRouche calls for in his Fourth Law, which is for a fusion driver, science-driver crash program, which includes the space program.

For that space program today, Krafft Ehricke is the absolute touchstone; he is the model of what a successful and meaningful space program for mankind must be. Krafft Ehricke was born one hundred years ago, in 1917, and he was there from the very beginning of the Space Age. He was born only a few years after mankind had first achieved flight, and he recalled that as a young man he was completely gripped by the idea that mankind could leave the Earth and open up a new world beyond the Earth; could bring civilization to take up residency in a completely new world, which was separate from the Earth.

This idea fascinated him. This is not merely the idea of extending terrestrial mankind and all of his existing qualities out to a different place, but *transforming* mankind by opening up a completely new world. Krafft Ehricke said that this could really only be compared to the event many millions, perhaps billions of years ago when life first emerged from the oceans onto land.

It is that magnitude of a change Krafft Ehricke was thinking about, and he took upon himself the responsibility for making those first steps happen.

The Extraterrestrial Imperative

So this is the idea of what a space program is really about; an idea much more advanced than almost all of Krafft Ehricke's contemporaries—and it is certainly much more advanced than what people today think. As a people, we have generally become somewhat demoralized, somewhat practical; we have submitted to the idea that we can only do small things. But Krafft was different. He was not looking for big victories in a space race against our enemy. He was not even looking for simple exploration where we send people millions and millions of miles away, to plant a flag somewhere and then come back and check it off of our list. He was not thinking of anything practical, except to the extent that it served this mission of mankind's extraterrestrial imperative.

That mission of the "extraterrestrial imperative," Krafft Ehricke saw as a fundamental transformation of mankind. I think you could make a comparison to that difference in thinking, if you think back to the European settlers who first crossed the Atlantic Ocean and came to America. Some of those people came here for reasons of adventure, seeking a fortune, or perhaps escaping something. Most of the people who came here came, in their own minds at least, for somewhat practical reasons.

However there was a minority of people who understood that the possibility of setting up a republic on the shores of America would *completely alter human history*. That's how Krafft Ehricke thought about the space program.

Now, what Krafft did—he had a shorter life than he should have had—but what he dedicated that life to, and what he worked on, especially in the last decade of his life, was how we would move every aspect of civilization off of the Earth, and how that would open up completely new possibilities for mankind, unveiling new potentialities of places like the Moon, for example. Krafft worked tirelessly to imagine what many of those new possibilities might be.

What he said, in a paper he wrote in, I think it was around 1955, was: We have to begin by occupying low-Earth orbit; we have to begin by putting a space station up into orbit. And he said we could do that by the 1960s. Now, as people know, we had Skylab in the 1970s, and the Mir space station a little later; we didn't get the full-fledged International Space Station until the 1990s. But Krafft said we could have a space station by the 1960s, and he imagined this would be the first baby step, the training ground for human beings to begin living and operating in space, to learn more about Man's biology and medical conditions; to do experimentation with how chemistry behaved in the space environment, how different materials behaved in the space environment, and so on.

He also imagined things that could be put into orbit around Earth, like hospitals or retirement homes. And I think that was very beautiful, because he was thinking about how in orbit you have a completely unique environment of zero-gravity, and of what new benefit zero-gravity could bring to people who are recovering from injuries; or how we could relieve the stress on the joints of people who are elderly by moving them to a lower-gravity environment.

Krafft also imagined that we would begin to set up manufacturing facilities in zero-gravity and take advantage of that unique environment, which could allow us to build structures of metal with a much higher purity, and stronger than we can manufacture on Earth. Krafft imagined space stations that would be resorts where people could go on vacation and experience a completely new environment, including a "zero-gravity swimming pool," where you could swim around as if in water. He imagines first conquering low-Earth orbit and then very quickly moving beyond, to absorb all of cis-lunar space—or the space that includes the Earth all the way up to the Moon and their orbits—into human civilization.

How did he think about that? I want to give one example from our pamphlet [**Figure 1**]. This is an image from the newest LaRouche PAC pamphlet, "La-

FIGURE 1

Days travel from New York City 1830 vs 1857
How rail transformed America's space-time relations

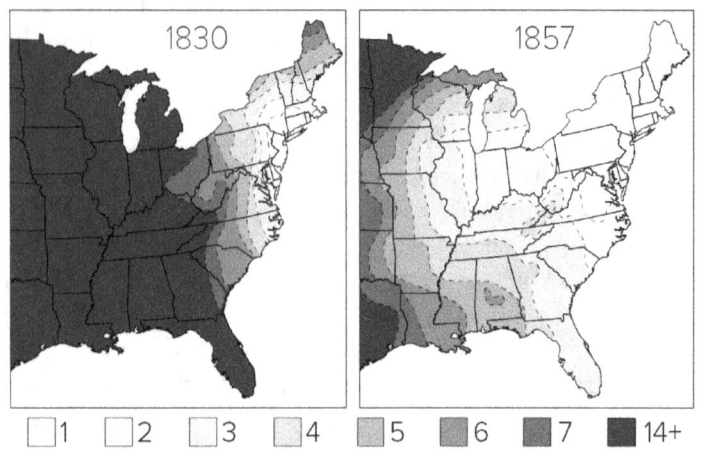

| ☐1 | ☐2 | ☐3 | ☐4 | ☐5 | ☐6 | ■7 | ■14+ |

Ben Deniston

Rouche's Four Laws & America's Future on the New Silk Road." It gives an example of how space-time was changed with the building of rail in the United States. What is indicated by the different colors is how many days of travel it would take from New York City to get to any of the other areas in the United States. Look at the transformation between 1830 and 1857, because of the building of rail: space and time became *condensed*—and this transformed everything, not just passenger travel, but it also completely changed the economic possibilities for moving freight, moving semi-finished products, moving raw materials to different industrial centers.

Krafft Ehricke imagined such a thing for cislunar space, and as part of his work, he thought of the design of a multi-layered transportation system that would incorporate different segments from the Earth to the Moon. In a 1984 paper, he called this the "Diana Fleet." Think about what the different components are of transportation between the Earth's surface and the Moon's surface. First, you have to get from the surface of the Earth up into low-Earth orbit. The way we do that today is with very large launch rockets, like the Saturn V rocket, or the one that NASA is building today, the SLS. There are more modern proposals for that today, which I won't go into. From low-Earth orbit, you must have vehicles to get to lunar orbit, for both people and freight, and then get from lunar orbit to the surface.

Here's something Krafft Ehricke designed [**Figure 2**], a nuclear-powered cargo ship. Krafft imagines that at a certain point in our process of developing the economic activity on the Moon, we will have a large fleet of nuclear-powered cargo ships that can move partially finished structures, raw materials like hydrogen, and other things, that would be imported from the Earth, and they can also transport materials from the Moon to the Earth.

Krafft also imagines some very novel ways of getting from lunar orbit to the lunar surface. Here is one that he designed himself, called the "Lunar Slide Lander" (LSL) [**Figure 3**]. The LSL would descend from orbit toward the surface, and would slow down by sliding along the sandy/gravelly surface of the Moon, which transfers the momentum of the ship to the lunar soil. Krafft points out

FIGURE 2

Krafft Ehricke

FIGURE 3

Krafft Ehricke

that by utilizing the unique features of the lunar surface in this way, you could reduce the amount of propellant that you would need for descent by 90 percent.

He also imagined new ways of getting from the surface of the Moon to lunar orbit using something he designed, which is basically a maglev launch system. It is a partially enclosed launch tube with a vehicle that would be propelled partially by electromagnets and partially by propellant, and in which much of the hydrogen expelled by the propellant could be recovered.

The Moon and LaRouche's Fourth Law

Krafft was thinking about how we could integrate this new, unique envi-

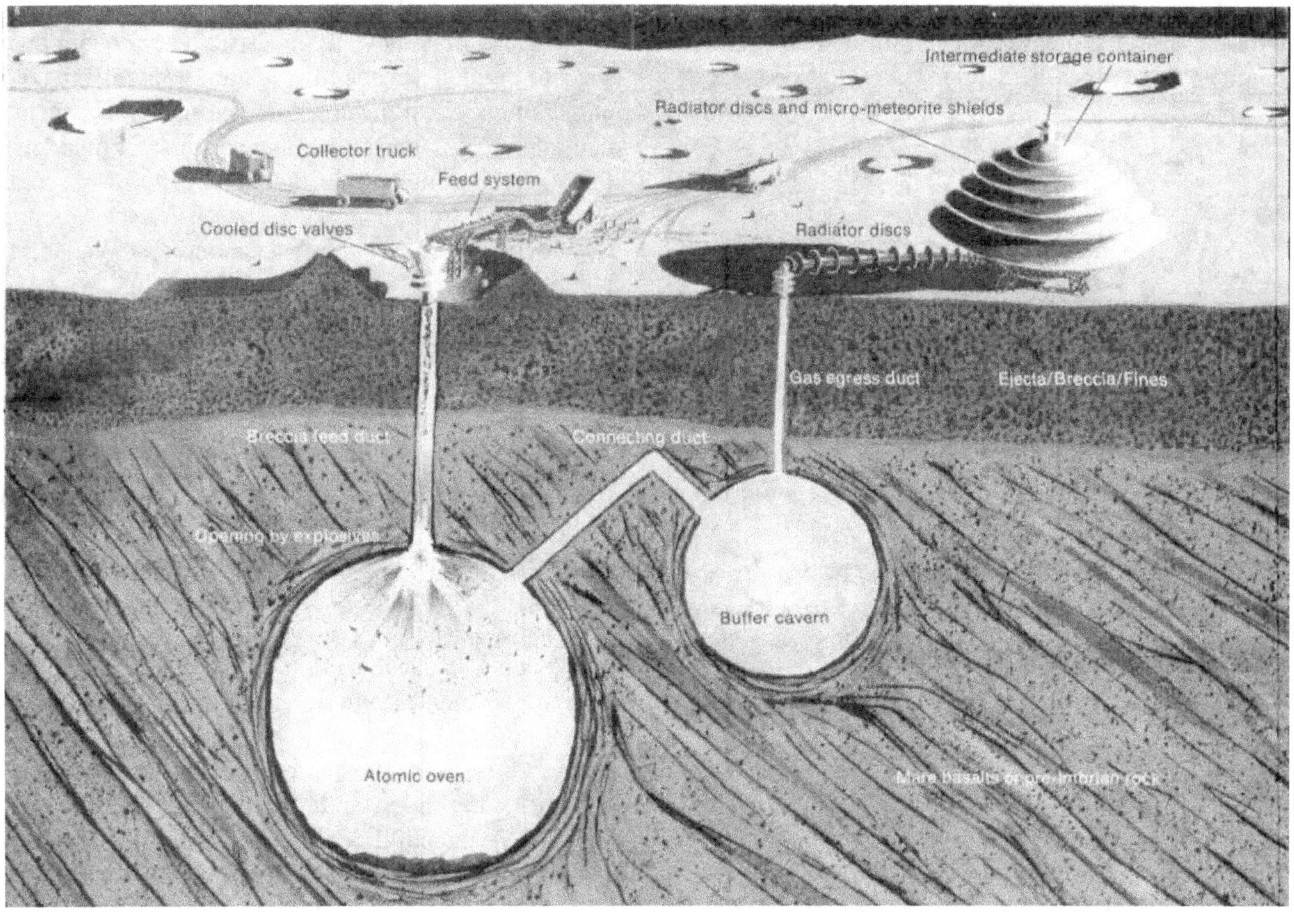

Krafft Ehricke

Krafft also imagined and designed a way to use nuclear explosions to mine and refine raw materials.

ronment into civilization, and how we can use mankind's actions, in leaving the Earth and going out into the Solar System, as a *driver* to develop new capabilities, new technologies. One thing he saw clearly is that for cislunar (nearby) space, nuclear-ion propulsion and chemical propulsion are completely adequate; but if we want to go farther, if we want to start from the Moon and go to Mars, or go to the moons of Jupiter— the kinds of things he describes in his story, "Expedition Ares"—we have to move quickly to a nuclear-powered rocket. I'm going to come back to that in a minute.

Another thing he thought of is the unique kinds of products that could be manufactured on the Moon. Until reading Krafft's works, I hadn't really considered what kinds of things you might manufacture on the Moon—I guess I had always thought of the Moon as the desolate frontier where we would just manufacture the bare necessities for people to live there; maybe we would make some ugly gray bricks to build some houses or something! But Krafft had a completely different idea: that with the resources on the Moon, and with the establishment of a central processing/manufacturing center on the Moon, you could produce an

incredible array of products! He said, on the Moon you could produce products such as sheet metal, trusses of aluminum, titanium and magnesium, casting bars, wires, glass, glass-wool, ceramics, powdered ceramics, insulation, silicon chips, and solar panels. You could also produce entire structures of various metals that would be needed to enlarge the lunar space station, for example, or to build fusion power plants on the Moon's surface. You could manufacture and build all of these things on the Moon. You could also manufacture water and liquid oxygen, which would be needed for chemical propellant and for life-support systems.

Another important thing he spoke of manufacturing on the Moon is helium-3. We know today, that you don't need to *manufacture* helium-3 on the Moon; you can just mine it from the lunar soil. The reason we want helium-3 is because it is the ideal fuel for fusion power. Krafft saw this as being not so much a *product,* but rather as an *outcome* of establishing civilization on the Moon: fusion power.

Fusion power plants are actually easier to establish on the Moon than they are on Earth. Not only are they easier to build, because of the natural vacuum and cold temperatures on the Moon (both needed for a fusion plant), but fusion power is also necessary for lunar civilization: you cannot power lunar civilization with solar panels! Aside from the low power density, the Moon is dark for two weeks out of the month! So you need fusion power to underwrite lunar civilization.

I think this is fascinating! Here we have been trying to achieve fusion power on Earth, since the 1940s and 1950s, but fusion might actually "belong" to civilization on the Moon.

I want to end with a thought from Lyndon LaRouche, which I think is very important. While we're reading this, I want you to think back to what I opened with: imagining mankind one hundred years from now, and what the meaning of 2017 *actually* is from their standpoint.

Lyndon LaRouche said, "All mankind has a commitment, an innate commitment, to create knowledge of the future… All mankind must subdue their passions to conform to what the future of mankind represents. The point is the understanding of the individual to reach and achieve the ability of insight into what the future species must do: the improvement of the human species! Lifting the human species out of its ordinary existence, taking it out of its mediocrities."

Space: The Ultimate Money Frontier

by Lyndon H. LaRouche, Jr.

This article was first published in the April 22, 2005 issue of EIR.

It was the fair mid-1970s estimate, that the U.S. economy had received about 14 cents in benefits from each penny which the U.S. Federal government had spent on the U.S. Manned Moon Landing program.[1] So much for those hyperventilating, glassy-eyed, Mont Pelerin Society fanatics, who chant endlessly, that we must get the Federal government out of the U.S. economy.

The following identifies summarily each of the five sets of facts which any competent economist would have considered as background, before rendering judgment on those issues of space policy which are identified in Marsha Freeman's report. First, the general dependency of all sustainable profitability of a national economy upon energy-intensive, capital-intensive modes of investment in scientific and technological improvements of the per-capita productive powers of labor. Second, the division of responsibility between government and the private sector in providing this investment. Third, why the government's investment in military and aerospace technology has proven itself to be such a big winner in the fight to increase the real national income of the U.S.A. Fourth, how the proposed Mars-colonization proposals of 1985-1986 came about, and how they will benefit the U.S. economy. Fifth, how space science works to this effect.

1. The American System of Political-Economy

The "American System of political-economy," as that term was defined by President George Washington's Treasury Secretary, Alexander Hamilton, was imposed, implicitly, as an integral feature of the U.S. Constitution's **Preamble** and *Article I*. At that time, 1787-1789, it was conceived, and received, as a remedy for the nearly fatal economic sickness of "free trade,"

with which the nation had been infected through the compromises embedded within the Articles of Confederation and in the 1782-1783 treaties with the United States' mortal adversary, then and now, the British monarchy.

It was the understandable zeal for peace with both Britain, and also with Britain's U.S. admirers, which had brought about the nearly fatal corruption pervading the 1783-1789 U.S.A. The compromise with Britain had been effected, first, during 1782, with Prime Minister William Fitzmaurice Petty and his creature, British Foreign Service head Jeremy Bentham.[2] The 1763-1783 stay-behinds are found among both the strata of wealthy slave-owners, which later formed the oligarchy of Britain's American puppet-state, the 1861-1865 Confederacy, and New England and Quaker Tories. The Tories of North Atlantic states were typified by the treasonous, leading U.S. agent of Jeremy Bentham's British foreign-intelligence service, Aaron Burr: those families which profitted from the slave-trade, from the British opium trade, and as London-loving textile manufacturers working in partnership with the purveyors of slave-produced cotton.[3]

---

1. See box, page 16.

2. The first of these agreements was negotiated with Prime Minister Shelburne (William Fitzmaurice Petty), during 1783. Initially, that agreement was repudiated by Shelburne's successors, but realities obliged them to affirm it in fact in the proceedings of the 1783 Treaty of Paris. The adoption of the "free trade" policies of the British East India Company, the interest which Shelburne represented, was the condition of peace imposed upon both France and the United States in the negotiation of these treaties.

3. On the subject of the common purpose of the two American tory oligarchies, the New England abolitionists and the Confederacy's slavemasters, see Anton Chaitkin, Treason in America, 2nd edition (New York: New Benjamin Franklin House, 1985); H. Graham Lowry, How The Nation Was Won, Vol. I (Washington, D.C.: Executive Intelligence Review, 1987); and, the work which influenced President Abra-

EIRNS/Stuart Lewis

Lyndon LaRouche addresses the Krafft Ehricke Memorial Conference on June 15, 1985. Out of discussions of LaRouche's presentation to that conference, the author was prompted to publish a proposal, in 1986, for a 40-year mission orientation for establishing a science colony on Mars. The concept was presented in the form of a Presidential-campaign television broadcast, "The Woman on Mars," in 1988. Inset: Krafft Ehricke at a New York City forum, Nov. 28, 1981.

EIRNS/Stuart Lewis

Protective Federal regulation of foreign and interstate commerce, a Federal government monopoly respecting the issuance and regulation of legal tender, a centralized common defense under Federal authority, the promotion of public works of infrastructure, and the fostering of scientific and technological progress in infrastructure, agriculture, and manufacturing, were leading considerations motivating, and reflected in the 1787-1789 Constitution.

This "American System," rooted in the economic and monetary successes of the pre-1689 Massachusetts Bay Colony, is the economic design famously associated with such names as Benjamin Franklin, Alexander Hamilton, the Careys, John Quincy Adams, Henry Clay, Friedrich List, E. Peshine Smith, and Abraham Lincoln's pre-Teddy Roosevelt Republican Party, and has proven itself the most successful model of economy which has been seen in any part of the world during the recent three centuries.

The United States, in particular, never had an economic depression, or kindred experience, during any part of the 1793-1995 interval, since Washington's first administration, which depression was not the result of

deviating from the U.S. Federal Constitution, into the follies of both "free trade" and kindred British corruptions of our national monetary, banking, and economic policies.

The Mont Pelerin Society quack-remedies peddled lately by fellows such as Senator Phil Gramm and Speaker Newt Gingrich, are not the cure; they are the disease, like the corrupting influence of famous American tories such as Albert Gallatin, or Andrew Jackson, Wall Street banker Martin van Buren, Franklin Pierce, treasonous President Buchanan, British spies Judah Benjamin and August Belmont, and, after Lincoln's murder, Andrew Johnson, Teddy Roosevelt, Woodrow Wilson, and Calvin Coolidge. Since 1763—and even earlier—there have been only two parties of principle in the United States, crossing all other nominal political-party lines: the patriotic party of Cotton Mather, Benjamin Franklin, Washington, Lincoln, and Franklin Delano Roosevelt, *versus* that tory tradition of Aaron Burr, the Massachusetts Lowells, and Benedict Arnold, which Americans in the Winston Churchill-loving tradition, such as Henry Kissinger, George Bush, Phil Gramm, Newt Gingrich, and the rabid "free trade" Democrats, typify today.

As documented in other locations, the characteristic of differences in way of thinking, which divides the pa-

ham Lincoln, Henry C. Carey, **The Slave Trade, Domestic & Foreign,** Reprint of 1858 edition (New York: Augustus M. Kelley, 1967).

triots from the American tories, still today, is that the governing principles of the tories, are typified by the empiricist world-outlook specific to the kind of philosophical liberalism (and, also, fascism) associated with Thomas Hobbes and John Locke.[4] That point is underscored by the contrast between preambles of the respective constitutions of the U.S.A. and the pro-slavery Confederacy. The tories are followers of Locke; whereas, the ideas of the U.S.A.'s patriotic founders were shaped by the explicitly anti-Locke influence of Gottfried Leibniz in physical science, in philosophy, in political morality, and in principles of political economy. Treasury Secretary Hamilton's famous, December 1791 Report to the U.S. Congress, **On The Subject of Manufactures,** illustrates the governing influence of Leibniz's economic science upon the American System of political-economy.

Putting to one side the expenditure for administrative and regulatory functions of the Federal government: Under the American System of political-economy, the dividing line between government's role in the economy, and that of the private entrepreneur, is essentially threefold: the government is responsible for the economy of national defense, the maintenance and development of basic economic infrastructure, and the promotion of progress and investment in advances in science and technology. In each case, the responsibility undertaken by, and assigned to government addresses a primary need of the economy which the sum-total of private entrepreneurs could not fulfill competently without government's own special and natural role in the economy of any civilized modern nation.

The responsibilities of government for infrastructure, include, presently, national and regional water management and related programs of general sanitation, public transportation, the organization of large-scale power grids, general urban infrastructure. This also includes governmental responsibility, at the variously appropriate levels of national, state, and local government, for a quality of universal education essential to the development of a qualified citizenry, and for the fostering of generalized increase of the productive powers of labor through investment in scientific and technological progress. It requires governmental responsibility, similarly, for ensuring the existence of ad-

4. Cf. Anton Chaitkin, et al., "The Anti-Newtonian Roots of the American Revolution," **EIR,** Dec. 1, 1995 and "Leibniz, Gauss Shaped America's Science Successes," **EIR,** Feb. 9, 1996. On the subject of "characteristic differences," see Lyndon H. LaRouche, Jr., "How Hobbes' Mathematics Misshaped Modern History," **Fidelio,** Spring 1996.

equate health-care delivery systems to all of the citizenry. It includes programs of scientific and technological progress which must be undertaken on a scale beyond the reasonable scope of the private entrepreneurs, as the Manhattan Project, the post-Sputnik program of National Science Foundation educational grants, and the Manned Moon-Landing program of the 1960s, typify this distinction.

2. The Lesson of the Soviet Union as an Infrastructure Desert

Go back to the second half of the 1960s. Compare three sets of national economies: A) The leading industrialized nations, typified by Japan, West Germany, and the United States; B) The Soviet bloc of nations (Eastern Europe and the Soviet Union); C) China and India as typical of greatly underdeveloped nations. Use maps of infrastructural features (rails, highways, inland waterways, and power grids) as aids in comparing the conditions in Japan and in Europe to the west of Berlin, with the development of infrastructure in continental Eurasia to the east and southwest of Berlin. Recognize, that during the second half of the 1960s, the general level of technology of production employed, and productivity, in Japan, the Federal Republic of Germany, and the U.S.A. were nearly equal, but that those three economies differed greatly in their respective population-densities per square kilometer of usable land-area. The characteristic of the three latter, developed economies, is the approximate functional correlation between population-density and density of infastructure development.

By contrast with those three developed economies, the Soviet Union fell far short of being competitive, by virtue of lack of adequate development of basic economic infrastructure. On the same premise, China and India were economic disasters.

The principle involved, is, summarily, as follows.

The most characteristic distinction, which sets the human race absolutely apart from, and above all other forms of life, is the quality of *cognition*: the ability of the individual human mind to create valid, revolutionary changes in axiomatic principles of human control over nature, by means of which the *potential relative population-density* of society is increased. This gain is reflected not only in an increase of the size and density of the human population, but also rises in individual life-expectancy, lowering of rates of sicknesses by age-interval group, and increases in both the "market basket" of household consumption and in the per-capita production of the contents of those household market-baskets.

Space Program Spending Paid for Itself Many Times Over

In April 1976, Chase Econometrics, a consulting firm associated with Chase Bank, released a study which estimated that for every $1 spent in the U.S. space program, $14 was returned to the economy in new jobs, new factories, and increased productivity from new technologies. The study also found that dollars spent by NASA were four times as effective in boosting the economy compared to other R&D spending, and that the effects in the economy of technology that had been developed by NASA were visible within two years of application.

There is no other *legal* activity that can claim that rate of return on investment.

While no listing of individual technology developments could add up to the economic impact of the mission to land men on the Moon, a survey does present examples of how such investments transform economic activity for the economy as a whole.

Agriculture: Observing the Earth from space has given farmers a tool with which to evaluate the health of crops, by determining infestation of pests, water stress, efficiency of fertilizers, and other factors. Threats to crops can be determined months before they would be visible from the ground, and action taken in time to avoid large-scale loss of food. Future applications of space technology in agriculture will include the use of automated and robotic systems being developed to grow food in Earth orbit and on other planets.

Medicine and health: Medical technologies that have benefitted from, or depended upon, NASA-funded research and development include fluid-flow studies for the artificial heart, miniaturized implantable insulin delivery systems for diabetics, remote monitoring of vital signs in intensive care units, rechargeable cardiac pacemakers, astronaut "cool suit" treatment for multiple sclerosis patients, implantable heart defibrillators, diagnostic tools and technologies, and thousands of other capabilities that have saved lives, improved the productivity of victims of many ailments, and helped prevent disease.

Energy: Many ideas for quantitative and qualitative improvements in energy technologies were initiated to enable the production of electricity under the constraints imposed by space flight and the space environment. They were under development to enable the colonization of the Moon, and travel to and development of Mars. Quantitative improvements included the development of compact, high-temperature nuclear fuel arrays for second-generation nuclear fission power plants. Qualitative breakthroughs centered around direct conversion techniques, such as applications of magnetohydrodynamics, and new energy production methods, notably, nuclear fusion.

Manufacturing: Industrial processes of every type have been pushed ahead through the use of new materials, computer control, non-destructive testing techniques, quality control methods, and thousands of individual innovations that were required in order to manufacture spacecraft that could withstand the space environment, and support both men and machines. Nastran, a computer software package, was developed at the NASA Goddard Space Flight Center during 1965-70, to analyze the behavior of elastic structures. In 1970, it was released for public use, and it was employed in aircraft and automobile manufacture, bridge construction, and power-plant modeling studies.

Transportation: The most significant increase in productivity in traditional transport systems, such as rail, since World War II, came from the application of computers. A dispatching and control system, originally developed by TRW for the Apollo guidance system, was adapted for ground transport, and used in the rail industry. Highly innovative transport technologies, from magnetically levitated vehicles to sub-orbital electromagnetic mass drivers, have benefitted from various space technologies, and will be deployed on a large scale on the Moon and Mars.

Scientists and engineers: During the 1960s, NASA provided the resources for thousands of college- and graduate-level students to pursue studies in science and engineering. Grants went to educational institutions to upgrade facilities, to faculty to support their research, and to students to encourage them to study the sciences. The peak year for NASA funding was 1965. The peak year for doctorates granted in the physical sciences (approximately 4,500) and in engineering (approximately 3,500), was in 1971, not because NASA paid for all of these degrees, but because there was great interest in joining in the space enterprise. At the start of the space program in 1960, the United States was graduating fewer than 2,000 Ph.D.s in the physical sciences. The number increased as NASA funding increased, and then declined, as NASA funding declined, with about a five-year lag time.   —*Marsha Freeman*

Until the late Eighteenth Century, the overwhelming majority of the populations of sundry cultures was rural. At the time of the first census of the U.S. population, for example, more than 90% were still rural. The technological development of farming, forestry, and mining, was the foundation of mankind's production of the physical preconditions of existence. In the history of the early colonies in North America, and the young United States, the transformation of a relatively unfruitful wilderness into fertile, developed farmlands, was the foundation of progress in the human condition. Hamilton's 1791 **On The Subject of Manufactures** provides a prophetic, rather detailed description of the process by means of which the United States was to be developed into the world's leading agro-industrial power.[5] It was the fostering of manufactures, made feasible through such means as development of roads and canals, which made feasible the interdependent increase in the productivity of agriculture and urban industry, as Hamilton describes this process. This development of infrastructure, is to be regarded as a development of the economic fertility of the entire inhabited land-area of the nation, comparable to the measures by which a fertile farm is hacked out of an infertile wilderness.

Hence, the relatively desert-like quality of infrastructural underdevelopment, and corresponding economic infertility, of most of the habitable territory of the former Soviet Union.

During the Nineteenth Century, the repertoire of basic economic infrastructure required, was expanded, to include railways, steam power, and so on. In the history of our Federal republic, infrastructure was supplied, chiefly, as either an economic activity of government, or through the instrumentality of privately owned, but government-regulated public utilities. This included not only tangible forms of infrastructure, but also the leading role of government in providing the means for universal education, health-care systems, and the fostering of science and technology.

Relatively speaking, an ironical failure of the Soviet economy, is that it lacked that "socialist" institution most successfully developed in capitalist western continental Europe, Japan, and the U.S.A.: publicly provided basic economic infrastructure, the indispensable development of the potential economic fertility of the land-area of the nation. Similarly, the conspicuous economic challenge facing nations such as China and India is, similarly, the development of a basic economic infrastructure adequate to foster urgently wanted increases in the potential productive powers of the nation's labor-force.

3. Military Spending and Space

Exploration as Infrastructure

In modern warfare, the per-capita effectiveness of the individual soldier depends upon the technology and related logistical support with which he and his unit are equipped.[6]

In the history of the United States, the premises of military achievement were the fostering of technological progress within the Federal arsenal system, combined with the civil engineering programs, copying those features of Gaspard Monge's 1794-1814 *Ecole Polytechnique* in France, at West Point and Annapolis. Under Presidents James Monroe and John Quincy Adams, the model for scientific development of the U.S. military capabilities was the military science-driver programs developed in France, by Monge and Lazare Carnot, during 1793-1814. Later, as post-1814 France's quality degenerated under the influence of Laplace, Cauchy, and the positivists, the U.S. national security apparatus, centered around Benjamin Franklin's great-grandson, Alexander Dallas Bache, turned to the Germany of Alexander von Humboldt and Carl F. Gauss for the shaping of U.S. scientific progress and related military programs.[7]

It should be noted, that Lazare Carnot assumed command of the military defense of France at a time when the British agents in Paris, Robespierre's Jacobins, were satisfied that the invading armies would soon effect the dismemberment of France.[8] Carnot, already

5. It should be stressed, that at the beginning of the Nineteenth Century, the average citizen of the United States had more than twice the literacy rate of the average subject in the British Isles, was approximately twice as productive, and had approximately double the standard of living. This advantage was not the "bounty of nature," but the fruit of combined educational policies and dedication to scientific and technological progress, beginning with the Seventeenth-Century Massachusetts Bay Colony.

6. The study of this development in modern warfare may be begun with reference to the relevant inventions of Leonardo da Vinci and the writings on warfare by Leonardo's ally Niccolò Macchiavelli.

7. See Anton Chaitkin, "Leibniz, Gauss Shaped America's Science Successes," *loc. cit.*

8. The direction of the French Jacobins was supplied from London by the Jeremy Bentham who had assumed direction of the British foreign

A CASPARD MONCE SES ELEVES ET SES CONCITOYENS MDCCCXLIX

wikipedia

Library of Congress Prints and Photographs Division

President John Quincy Adams. "Under Presidents James Monroe and John Quincy Adams, the model for scientific development of the U.S. military capabilities was the military science-driver programs developed in France, by Monge and Lazare Carnot, during 1793-1814."

established as a genius in military science, and also a ranking scientist, assembled his friends of the Monge circle to effect a technological revolution in warfare, as part of his rebuilding the French military forces under his command. The deployment of newly designed mobile field artillery, and its use for massed artillery fire, was among the measures which revolutionized warfare. Under the Lazare Carnot who came to be celebrated as the "Author of Victory," French forces went, during months, from effective defense to appearing as the virtually irresistable military force of the continent of Europe, creating the great instrument so famously

misused by the picaresque Napoleon Buonaparte. The intertwined efforts of the two collaborators, Carnot and the Ecole Polytechnique's Monge, established the model for what later efforts, such as the Manhattan Project and the German-American space-program, identify as science-driver forms of "crash programs."

Although we might trace the origins of the modern science-driver "crash program" to the Platonists Archimedes and Leonardo da Vinci, the conception of such programs is traced directly to Gottfried Leibniz's specifications for a science of physical economy, as developed through the work of such explicitly anti-Newton followers of Leibniz as the French 1793-1814 science community associated with Carnot and Monge.

During the Twentieth Century, most of the technological progress which has occurred, would not have occurred but for the impetus supplied by perceived military-strategic imperatives. Although space exploration lies as much outside the domain of military expenditure as within, the mid-1950s "moth-balling" of a Hunts-

---

intelligence service under Lord Shelburne. For example, the French Danton and the Swiss lunatic Marat, were both trained personally by Bentham, in London, and sent to France to take over leadership of the Jacobin Terror. The relevant point, in this text location, is that the assigned function of the Jacobins was not to lead France, but to arrange its destruction. Carnot was given leadership of the military, not to secure its success, but to assume the blame for a defeat which was presumed to be inevitable at that time.

ville capability for putting a satellite into orbit, typifies the ugly reality of our Hobbesian age. Had the Eisenhower administration been able to reach an "off" button, to stop the nagging beep of the Soviet Sputnik, put into orbit on Oct. 4, 1957, the U.S. space program would have been virtually choked to death by Arthur Burns' monetarist mothballs before the 1960s arrived.

For related reasons, the machine-tool activity centered in the arsenals has been the principal motor-force of modern investment in scientific and technological advances, in both improved qualities of products and increased productive powers of labor. Thus, although military products are essentially economic waste, throughout modern history, the greatest progress in the national income of nations has been won through that proliferation of new technologies which has occurred as a by-product of military investments in science and technology. As the Chase Econometrics study implies, government investment in space exploration has been the outstanding profit-producer for the taxpayer.

4. The 1985-1986 Mars-Colonization Program

My widely debated, 1985-1986 proposal for a 40-year mission orientation for planting a science colony on Mars, was prompted by Helga Zepp LaRouche's reaction to the December 1984 death of a dear friend and outstanding space-scientist, Dr. Krafft Ehricke. She assigned me to prepare a paper for delivery to an international scientific conference, convened in memory of Krafft, at Reston, Virginia, June 15-16, 1985.[9] Out of discussions of my presentation during that conference, I was prompted to produce the proposal which I presented for publication about six months later, at the beginning of 1986. That proposal attracted much wider recognition, and a still-raging controversy, when it was presented in the form of a half-hour presidential-campaign television broadcast, "The Woman on Mars," during 1988.

The manner in which this came about typifies the general rule in modern science. It is an account which need be told, if one is to understand the policy-framework within which U.S. space-policy is situated today.

True to the Twentieth-Century intertwining of military procurement and space science, my association with space-science, and my approach to space explora-

tion had developed as a result of my contribution to what President Ronald Reagan named the "Strategic Defense Initiative" (SDI). I had first published that SDI design during August 1979, as a document of my 1980 campaign for the Democratic Party's Presidential nomination. That was brought into the Reagan administration through my 1982-1983 work, on behalf of certain Reagan administration agencies, in exploratory, back-channel discussions with the Soviet government.

One must glance back, to events few years earlier, to understand how this came about.

My own work in this direction had begun during 1975-1976. It started when I encountered a leaked report in the Hamburg newsweekly, **Der Spiegel,** on a pending NATO desk-operation of the Hilex series. This strange **Spiegel** report drew my attention to a piece of insanity which, I soon came to discover, was officially denoted as proposed NATO doctrine MC-14/4. These facts prompted my conviction that the developments in solid-fuel boosters and precision of targeting, combined with the urge toward forward-basing, were bringing us toward the threshold of potential first-strike nuclear warfare. When heads of superpowers are faced with the detection of a clutch of missiles a few minutes from one's territory, and the prospect that those few missiles might be capable of "pinning down" one's ability to kick back, the world were at the brink of a "first nuclear strike" potential. *Without an effective strategic ballistic-missile defense,* "first strike" would cease to be an unlikely strategic option.

The next step toward the idea which was to become known as SDI, was some 1977 discussions, held on my behalf, with the then recently retired, former head of Air Force intelligence, Maj.-Gen. George Keegan. Keegan suggested that scientists associated with me assess the evidence that the Soviet Union had the capability of developing a deployable, ground-based, ballistic-missile defense based upon what the 1972 ABM-treaty suffixes identify as "new physical principles." Keegan's concerns parallelled my own, in opposition to the regrettably stubborn, anti-scientist prejudices of former DIA head and (1980s) Heritage Foundation associate Daniel P. Graham.[10]

_____

9. "Ehricke's Contribution to Global and Interplanetary Civilization," Proceedings of the Schiller Institute's Krafft Ehricke Memorial Conference, June 15-16, 1985, **Colonize Space!** (New York: New Benjamin Franklin House, 1985), pp. 27-51.

_____

10. During late 1982, until after March 23, 1983, Lieutenant-General (ret.) Graham was a vigorous opponent of the policy which became the SDI. Even after he came around to professing support for the SDI by name, he insisted upon stressing "off-the-shelf" and related "kinetic energy" systems, deprecating "new physical principles," as he had during his earlier attacks upon me and Dr. Edward Teller.

My standpoint was different than many among the U.S. strategists who came to agree with the SDI simply as a sane choice of military technology. Winston Churchill's Britain had been all too successful in exploiting—early and often—the premature death of Churchill's deadly political opponent, Franklin Delano Roosevelt. Churchill's London had lured Washington and Moscow into that geopolitical balance-of-superpowers game, by means of which the tattered and smelly remains of the old British Empire could play off Moscow and Washington to London's profit, using the superpower conflict as a means of subordinating the sovereignty of every nation on this planet, to London's manipulating the relations between the two superpowers.

Unfortunately, by the late 1970s, very few among the relevant professionals, barring a relative handful of exceptions in Europe, recognized the significance of the fundamental strategic conflict between Roosevelt and Churchill. They did not comprehend the fundamental strategic significance of such follies of Averell Harriman's and Winston Churchill's Harry Truman, as Truman's firing and fraudulent defamation of Gen. Douglas MacArthur, an action which brought to an end the United States' true sovereignty as a nation-state, and ushered in those immoral forms of "cabinet" warfare pioneered in post-MacArthur Korea, and applied with a vengeance in 1960s Southeast Asia. So, by the late 1970s and early 1980s, only a dwindling handful among our military understood what was evil in Robert S. McNamara's and Henry Kissinger's pushing the Russell-Szilard, Pugwash dogmas of "détente."

My starting-point, was to view the mutuality of the danger posed by trends of both powers toward forward basing, as a premise for bringing about a strategically indispensable, axiomatic change in global economic policy. Since *effective* forms of strategic ballistic-missile defense could not be accomplished by any means less advanced than "new physical principles," U.S.-Soviet agreement to cooperation in developing such a strategic missile defense, could, in my estimate, not merely bring the immediate military problem increasingly under control, but would represent an international science-driver effort, which would accelerate the productive powers of labor throughout the planet, through the "spillovers" of military technology into the civilian economies of the world as a whole.

It was on that point that Dr. Edward Teller's 1982 references to use of these technologies to advance "common aims of mankind," and the offer of techno-

logical cooperation featured in President Reagan's March 23, 1983 announcement, coincided precisely with my views on the proper design of the proposed agreement between the superpowers.

These global economic implications of effective strategic defense, were the point of departure for my 1985-1986 development of the Mars-colonization proposal. My views on the military and political-economic impact of "new physical principles" approaches to strategic defense, were, and are central axioms of my Mars-colonization program.

The crucial strategic incompetence which General Graham and his factional allies would never overcome, was their inability to recognize that it is economically impossible to achieve assured preponderance of the strategic defense by use of "kinetic energy" means, within the domain of dense flotillas of rocket-launched nuclear warheads. One must change the geometry of that domain, the aerial battlefield, a change in the physical geometry of the problem, which only "new physical principles" could accomplish. In the political-strategic domain, the same principle prevailed: Peace could be achieved only through either the defeat, or collapse of one of the superpowers, or through a radical change in the political-economic geometry of the planet. The same "new physical principles," properly applied in a coordinated way, would accomplish the optimal result in both respects.

That is the quality of scientific and strategic thinking which is indispensable for competent formulation of space policy.

During 1982, my exploratory back-channel discussions with Moscow representatives, were parallelled by my briefings to relevant scientific and military institutions of other nations, including France, Germany, Italy, India, and Japan, on the type of policy which I was proposing (of course, without referencing my back-channel discussions with Moscow). Numerous among these professionals had significant backgrounds in space science and related fields. A wide assortment of valuable collaborators was brought together in this fashion. This activity overlapped the significant scientific competencies of the Fusion Energy Foundation, of which I have been a co-founder, and with which I was actively involved throughout the period. Out of this aspect of the work on what became known as SDI, came the foundations for the 1985-1986 design of the Mars-colonization program.

My 1985-1986 Mars-colonization policy was developed and promulgated to prompt the U.S.A., as then still the leading nation of this planet, to use its leadership position to launch a global economic-recovery program whose design was based upon the lessons of the marvelous economic success of the 1960s Manned Moon Landing "crash program."

The need for such a program was great, even within the United States itself. By the close of the 1970s, the United States had lost critical, large chunks of that technology, which we had had during the 1960s, which had been indispensable for the 1969 success of the Apollo program. Today, during the past thirty years, the per-capita *physical* value of the United States' economy has been shrinking at an average rate of more than 2% per year.[11] Around the world, moving from nation to nation, one of the most consistent pictures of the past thirty years economic history, is the vanishing of entire, vital sectors of technology and of those types of labor skills which would be indispensable in any effort at an actual economic recovery. In short, contrary to the prophecies of such loonies as Britain's Lord William Rees-Mogg, and his American protégés Alvin Toffler and Newt Gingrich, the human body can not live on a diet of software.

The need for such a Mars colonization policy is much greater today, than during the mid-1980s. Without a very large-scale, government-based, global "crash program" form of science-driver spur to global investment in advanced technologies, it will be virtually impossible to effect an early general recovery of this planet's ruined economies. The revival of lost machine-tool and labor-skills resources, the stimulus to reviving educational systems from their presently technologically and culturally moribund condition, require, on an expanded scale, the kind of stimulus which was provided by the crash aerospace program of the mid-1960s.

5. The Economic principles of Space Science

It is not sufficient to rely only upon the practical politics of the attention-getting fact, that there was a fairly

estimated 14 cents return to the U.S. economy for each penny spent on the U.S. government's Kennedy space program. Just as a physician must prescribe no medication whose efficient principle is not known scientifically, costly governmental investments should not be risked on the opinions of political pragmatists. Since the relevant principles are presented in a significant number of published writings on my original discoveries in the science of physical economy, a summary suffices here.

The formal solution to the relevant, central problem of measurement in economic science, is set forth implicitly in Prof. Bernhard Riemann's widely circulated, but rarely understood habilitation dissertation of 1854.[12] To reduce any validated experimental discovery of physical principle to the appropriate form, that principle must modify the relevant set of axiomatic assumptions underlying the mathematical physics existing prior to that discovery. The result of such a modification of such a set of axioms, is what Plato, and scientists after him, Riemann included, identify by the term *hypothesis.* The formal product of applying any such hypothesis to a system of formal logic, such as a deductive mathematics, is an open-ended set of mutually consistent propositions, called *theorems,* constituting what is known as a *theorem-lattice.*

The relevant problem of hypothesis, which is central to economic science: Any change in the set of axioms underlying a theorem-lattice, produces a new theorem-lattice, none of whose theorems is consistent with any theorem of the previous lattice. Nonetheless, in every case of a valid discovery of principle, the result of the change in mathematical physics is measurable *in some way,* but not formally deducible from the standpoint of the old mathematics. What may be measured to such effect, is either a magnitude of extension, or, in the alternative, the clearly defined existence of the kind of mathematical discontinuity which marks the presence of what we term a *singularity.* In consequence of the preceding work of Carl F. Gauss, Riemann classified the general idea of those changes in yardsticks, brought about through valid experimental discoveries of physical principle, as *curvature* of physical space-time. The

---

11. The portion of this which is most readily measured, is shown by determining the increase in employment required to bring the output of each agricultural sector or industry up to the level of output needed to supply the same market-basket of goods, per household, which was average during the second half of the 1960s. In addition, we must consider the large amount of net disinvestment which has occurred in basic economic infrastructure and in productive and other physical capital goods of farms, industries, municipalities, and households, amounts which are not reflected in the deductions made by the Federal Reserve and government agencies, to arrive at estimated national Value Added. For these and additional reasons, the official estimates of National Product and National Income are essentially fraudulent, wildly overestimated.

---

12. Bernhard Riemann, *"Über die Hypothesen, welche der Geometrie zu Grunde liegen"* ("On the Hypotheses Which Underlie Geometry"), **Bernhard Riemann's Gesammelte Mathematische Werke,** Reprint of 1902 Teubner edition (New York: Dover Publications, 1953). See, Lyndon H. LaRouche, Jr., "Non-Newtonian Mathematics for Economists," **EIR,** Aug. 11, 1995.

term "curvature" is employed there in the same sense, that consistent errors in measurement of the shadows of sundials led to Eratosthenes' fair estimate of the curvature of the Earth's surface, about twenty-three centuries past.[13]

The relevance of Riemann's treatment of the metrical problem of hypothesis to economic science, is located in the essential distinction which sets man as absolutely superior to, and apart from all other forms of life. Man is the only species which can willfully increase its potential relative population-density, to such an effect that no principle of animal ecology can be applied competently to the study of human populations. We increase our species' potential relative population-density through that developable agency of the individual human intellect, which we recognize in such forms of expression as validated discovery of a new, higher principle of nature (i.e., the generation of a new hypothesis). The increase of potential relative population-density, is the yardstick used to measure those changes in the "curvature" of physical-economic space-time resulting from such efficient kinds of discoveries withn the domains of art and science.

We assimilate the individual such discoveries of other persons, by reenacting the original discoverer's mental experience of making that discovery, within our own minds. These mental processes, by which individuals make, or reenact original, valid discoveries in art and science, are recognizable by the term *cognition*. The term cognition, so defined in practice, is equivalent to the alternative term *creative reason*, creative reason as distinct from the qualitatively inferior mental activity of mere logic. The understanding which we acquire through those processes of cognition, constitutes that which deserves, uniquely, the term *knowledge*, as distinct from either sense-perception, mere deduction, or mere opinion. In other words, knowledge is limited to our accumulation of that body of valid original discoveries which we have made our own through either original discovery, or by reenacting the mental experience of original discovery.

This accumulation of knowledge is of the Riemann

form of a series in which each given level of discoveries of principle, up to some point, designated by *n*, is superseded by an additional such discovery, designatable as the *(n+1)'th* discovery (dimension). The series of many hypotheses which is generalized by the symbology *(n+1)/n*, is a series whose transfinite quality is what Plato designates by the term *higher hypothesis*, or *Becoming*.

The validity of that series, as demonstrable by measurement according to the principle of curvature, is the demonstration that the universe is so designed, that nature is obliged to obey those individual powers of cognition which produce, or act upon the directing premise of valid discoveries of higher principle. This is usefully restated: The human species' manifest ability to increase its potential relative population-density practically, through successive breakthroughs in scientific and related knowledge, demonstrates, *experimentally*, that the universe is so designed, that its laws are expressed in the form of generalized human cognition, human creative reason, of cognition in the form of higher hypothesis.

From those considerations, we derive the following framework governing the principles of space science.

In the universe we encounter three distinct qualities of processes. Proceeding from lower to higher, these three are: those processes we deem non-living, those we recognize as living, and the processes of cognition. None of the characteristics of the higher processes can be derived in a formal way from the characteristics of the lower processes. Among these three, what Leibniz identified as the notion of universal characteristics, are adumbrated for all three domains by the principles of cognitive processes.

The limitations of our senses also apportion the universe in which these three qualities of processes interact, among three domains: microphysics, astrophysics, and macrophysics, the latter corresponding to processes which can be examined directly on the scale of the senses. Also, there is an order in the succession of relatively valid new hypotheses, an order fairly identified by the notion of an ordering of "necessary predecessors" and "necessary successors," in the sequence of valid discoveries of principle in art and science.

From applying these considerations of economic science to exemplary experience with fruitful "crash programs" from the past, the general notion of a successful design for a structurable "science driver" form of new "crash program" may be derived. The work of the Monge Ecole Polytechnique, the Manhattan Proj-

---

13. Determine the meridian by obvious stellar observations. Place a series of sundials at intervals along that meridian, in a south to north direction. The measurement of the change in noon-time angle of the sunlight's shadow, leads to estimates of the curvature of the Earth's surface, and hence the size of the Earth. By including the case of singularities, we are able to state that some kind of measurement is always available for recognizing a valid discovery of physical principle.

ect, and the Kennedy space program, are prominent among the convenient examples.

Firstly, the subsuming objective of any science-driver "crash program," must be to increase mankind's power, per-capita, over the universe. This objective inheres in the principles of such a program, as summarily identified, immediately above. Thus, axiomatically, any such space program will produce immediate benefits for mankind on Earth.

Secondly, the immediate objective of such a "crash program" is not one or several valid discoveries of principle, but an entire family of such discoveries. This means, that one has chosen as a central target for such discovery an issue which A) is within the reach of constructable experimental measurements, B) involves each and all of the six phases of nature identified above,[14] C) brings together a wide array of discoveries which must be resolved as the necessary predecessors for the centrally targetted discovery of the project as a whole, D) identifies a direction for later, further central objects of discovery, which are made reachable through realizing the initial centrally targetted discovery.

The primary objective of the 1985-1986 Mars-colonization project, was, and still is a broad-based family of fundamental and successive scientific breakthroughs which will revolutionize the practice of science and technology on Earth.

The highlights of the program are as follows:

The immediate target, to be reached within an estimated forty years lapsed time, is the establishment of a permanent "science city" colony on Mars, serving space research as the science city of Los Alamos served the Manhattan project: a base of operations as far distant from the noisy Sun as is reasonable within such a time-span. This "science city" on Mars is to provide a forward base of operations for very-large-aperture arrays and related research tools, for the intensive study of every designated crucial variety of physical anomaly in space which might be accessed by apparatus set into space near Mars orbit.

The preliminary steps to be completed as prerequisites for establishing a permanent base on Mars, are: 1) Establishing a family of Earth-orbitting space-stations; 2) Achieving radical economies in bringing weight to space-station orbit, through replacement of direct ground-to-orbit rocket, by an approach modelled upon the Sänger project;[15] 3) Establishing "automated industrial" activities on the Moon, as envisaged for the U.S.A. by such veterans of Hermann Oberth's original Moon-landing program as Krafft Ehricke; 4) The fabrication of the heavy components of interplanetary vehicles and of Helium-3 fuel components in industrial facilities on the Moon; 5) The establishment of occasional and then regular flights of flotillas of interplanetary space-craft between Earth-orbit and Mars-orbit, combined with the reorientation of space-exploration to operations based upon this Earth-Mars link. And, so on.

In conclusion, three additional points are to be summarized. First, there is virtually no instance of any observatories or probes sent into solar space, which did not provoke the discovery of at least one crucial-experimental quality of anomaly. The universe is heavily populated with astrophysical anomalies which we know to exist, but want the means to examine in a more efficient way. On this basis, alone, the number of new fundamental discoveries awaiting mankind from even the preliminary next steps toward Mars colonization is awesomely large; these anomalies alone would assure us of numerous major scientific breakthroughs in the practice of science upon Earth. Second, no principle of nature is proven, until it is demonstrated experimentally in respect to all three domains of astrophysics, microphysics, and macrophysics, and in respect to the characteristics of both non-living and living processes. From the remotest beginnings of scientific knowledge, in the ancient construction of solar astronomical calendars, long before riparian silt deposits produced lower Mesopotamia, astrophysics has been the origin of man's mastery of the principles of scientific knowledge. Without astrophysics, microphysics could not have been developed, nor a rational macrophysics rendered possible. It remains the same today.

Man yearns upward, toward the exploration of space, for one overriding purpose: the fuller development of mankind on Earth.

---

14. I.e., non-living, living, cognitive processes, each and all examined on the scales of microphysics, astrophysics, and marcophysics.

15. The developed proposals for carrying out Eugen Sänger's design envisaged the pickabacking of a rocket plane upon the back of an approximately B-747-sized scramjet of between Mach 6 and Mach 8 capability. Since the scramjet would scavenge the heavier portion of its fuel—oxygen—from the air through which it travelled, the ratio of fuel consumption to net payload of the paired scram and rocketplane could be on the order of ten times as efficient as rocket ascent alone. This factor of cost is one of the prime barriers to reasonable economy and security in operations into nearby space.

All the News 'Unfit to Print'

by Rachel Brown

Apr. 9—The *New York Times,* ABC, CNN, FOX, and many other media outfits which claim to "report the news," seem to have reversed the old *New York Times* motto, making it today, "All the News un-fit to print." Amidst numberless stories of social decay and replays of late-night television, coverage of current politics has become inseparable from Hollywood gossip. News and entertainment have together become an intermeshed single display of degeneracy, all proclaiming the cynical, British-spawned viewpoint from which one is to view all social behavior and current events. Headline opinions are re-echoed by political leaders, providing at least a sort of coherence to the pseudo-reality occupied by a small group of our nation's "intellectual leadership," and presented to the public as "current reality."

The actions of the current president—who has rejected fundamental keystones of that British-run "reality," and has demonstrated a clear intention to resurrect the American System principles of national economy—are not only considered not "fit to print," but also therefore make him a fit target for destruction and removal. The following recent developments and speeches made by the President, are a small indication of the reasons that the British have launched a coup against his presidency, through political-intelligence operations such as the recent fraud perpetrated on the President regarding the use of chemical weapons in Syria.

On Monday, March 31, President Trump signed an Executive Order establishing the "President's Commission on Combatting Drug Addiction and the Opioid Crisis." The Commission will be chaired by Gov. Chris Christie, and will attempt to address the "scourge of drug abuse, addiction, and the opioid crisis." At the signing, the President stated:

I made a promise to the American people to take action to keep drugs from pouring into our country and to help those who have been so badly affected by them. Drug cartels have spread their deadly industry across our nation, and the availability of cheap narcotics, cheap narcotics—some of it of it comes in cheaper than candy—has devastated our communities. It's really one of the biggest problems our country has, and nobody really wants to talk about it. Vice President Pence mentioned this coming into the room,—he said, "this is a problem nobody understands," and I think they're going to start to understand. And more importantly, we have to solve the problem.

Our Attorney General Jeff Sessions is working very hard on this problem. It takes a lot of his time, because this causes so much of the crime that we have to solve, that problem. So solving the drug crisis will require cooperation across government and across society, including early intervention to keep America's youth off this destructive path. We must work together, trust each other, and forge a true partnership based on the common ground of cherishing human life.

creative commons
Mexican soldiers eradicating a poppy crop.

Coincident with the establishment of this new commission, the Mexican army allowed the U.S. military, for the first time in at least a decade, to observe opium poppy eradication in Mexico. U.S. military leaders and UN officials were flown by helicopter into drug eradication sites in Sinaloa and Chihuahua, two of the areas that make up the Golden Triangle where most Mexican opium is produced. This is a step toward deeper cooperation with the Mexican army in fighting the heroin traffickers.

On Tuesday, April 4, President Trump emphasized the unique historical role of our nation's builders and craftsmen, in an address to the 2017 North America's Building Trades Unions National Legislative Conference. He said:

I'm calling on all Americans—Democrat, Republican, independent—to come together and take part in the great rebuilding of our country.

That is why, in my address to Congress, I called on lawmakers to pass legislation that produces a $1-trillion investment in the infrastructure of our country. And we need it. With your help, we can rebuild our country's bridges, airports, seaports, and water systems. We will streamline the process to get approvals quickly, so that long-delayed projects can finally move ahead. And with lower taxes on America's middle class and businesses, we will see a new surge of economic growth and development.

All of you have come to the nation's capital to call members of the House and Senate to action. You've also called your President to action. When you see them, you can tell Congress that America's building trades and its President are very much united.

Together, we are ready to break new ground. We will build in the spirit of one of the great projects in our nation's history—an enduring symbol of American strength. The Empire State Building was forged in the Great Depression, and provided jobs for more than 3,000 workers. We've all seen the pictures—rugged workers perched dozens and dozens of stories up in the air. Workers like these moved almost 60,000 tons of steel, installed 200,000 cubic feet of stone, and laid 10 million bricks to build that American icon. And they did the job in a record time—13 months. Hard to believe. Think of that—the Empire State Building built in 13 months, during the Depression.

Construction workers building the Empire State Building.

wikilinks

Nowadays, you couldn't even get a building permit or approval in that amount of time. When the workers had secured the last piece of steel in that amazing and beautiful structure, they marked the moment—as we still do today—with what is called a "topping out" ceremony: 1,050 feet above the streets of New York City, they hoisted a beautiful and great American flag. It was an American flag that represented American projects—the big, bold, and daring dream of one man, and then one city, and then finally, one people. That banner marked our nation's proud climb to the top of the world. Our people endured through the hardships of Depression and the battles of World War II, and they emerged from these trials stronger and more united than ever before. Now, we must again summon that same national greatness to meet the challenges of our time.

Only miles from the halls of Congress and the newsrooms of Washington, you will find once-thriving cities marred by empty lots and once-booming industrial towns that have become rusted and are in total disrepair. Standing before me today, in this very hall, are the men and women who, if given the chance, can transform these communities. You are the citizens who can rebuild our cities, revive our industries, and renew our beloved country. And I know you will stop at nothing to get the job done.

For the rest of their lives, everyone who worked on the Empire State Building knew when they looked up at that great New York skyline that they had lifted the Stars and Stripes atop the tallest flagpole on Earth, and that somewhere high above the city streets, their place in history was carved into beams of steel.

In the future, when we overcome the trials—and we are in the trials of our times—we too will emerge stronger and more united than ever before. It's happening, you watch. When we rise above the cynics and critics who live only to defend the status quo, and to defend themselves from failure, then we, too, will construct a lasting monument to national greatness.

In this future, our nation's workers and craftsmen will look way out at the vast open landscape, and they will build new bridges and new schools and new landmarks, and they will proudly raise up for all to see our bright and beautiful American flag. And when we see that flag, we will remember that we all share one American home, one American heart, and one American destiny.

Should these developments become successful in their intentions, that is, the eradication of the London-run international drug trade, and the revival of the American System of political-economy—which carries with it implicit international collaboration with relevant nations—the British Empire would be finished. Remember that, next time the media tells you something.

Every Day Counts In Today's Showdown To Save Civilization

That's why you need EIR's **Daily Alert Service**, a strategic overview compiled with the input of Lyndon LaRouche, and delivered to your email 5 days a week.

The election of Donald Trump to the Presidency of the Untied States has launched a new global era whose character has yet to be determined. The Obama-Clinton drive toward confrontation with Russia has been disrupted--but what will come next?

Over the next weeks and months there will be a pitched battle to determine the course of the Trump Administration. Will it pursue policies of cooperation with Russia and China in the New Silk Road, as the President-Elect has given some signs of? Will it follow through against Wall Street with Glass-Steagall?

The opposition to these policies will be fierce. If there is to be a positive outcome to this battle, an informed citizenry must do its part--intervening, educating, inspiring. That's why you need the EIR Daily Alert more than ever.

TUESDAY, NOVEMBER 22, 2016

Volume 3, Number 65

EIR Daily Alert Service

P.O. Box 17390, Washington, DC 20041-0390

- Only Global Solutions, Based on New Principles, Can Work
- Tulsi Gabbard Meets with Donald Trump Regarding Syria
- Robert Kagan Throws in the Towel, Complains U.S. Is Becoming 'Solipsistic'
- War Party Moving To Preempt Trump-Putin Reset
- Syrian Army Makes More Progress in Aleppo
- Duterte Gives OK to Nuclear Power for Philippines
- Europe Will Suffer from Maintaining Russia Sanctions
- Former Chilean Diplomat Confirmed, 'We Will Joyfully Welcome Xi Jinping'
- Duterte and Putin Establish Philippines-Russia Cooperation
- François Fillon, Pro-Russian Thatcherite, Wins First Round of French Right-Wing Presidential Primary

EDITORIAL

Only Global Solutions, Based on New Principles, Can Work

II. The New World Constellation

British Coup Against Trump Overshadows U.S.-China Summit

by William Jones and Tony Papert

April 11—Millions of people in many countries had been looking with hope towards the April 6-April 7 summit of President Trump with China's President Xi Jinping. And they were right in their hopes. Not only was this to be a meeting between the leaders of the world's two largest economies. More to the point, President Trump had promised a trillion-dollar program to rebuild U.S. infrastructure, while China is actually the world's leading infrastructure power. China also holds a trillion dollars of U.S. Treasury bonds which could be invested to create jobs in the United States, and there has been high-level discussion in China of doing just that.

Still more important, China is in the middle of other earth-shaking developments which have been totally blocked out of the U.S. media. In 2013, President Xi inaugurated a Chinese initiative for a massive, cooperative world infrastructure program. That program, the "Belt and Road Initiative," is now ten times larger than the postwar Marshall Plan in real terms, and involves 70 countries. It is the wave of the future, and the United States must join it.

But a foreign hand intervened, and the April 6-April 7 summit was overshadowed by the course of a British coup-in-process against President Trump. The British tricked President Trump into striking Syria before any serious investigation; they intend to keep tripping him up, forcing him to stumble into near-term war with Russia—which will also mean war with China. They want to destroy Trump's plans for cooperation with Russia and China, and for his plans for anti-British

Xinhua/Lan Hongguang

President Trump (left) and President Xi Jinping (right) during their second round of talks April 7, 2017.

"American System" reforms in the United States—even if the British destroy the human race along the way.

This British coup can and must be stopped and reversed. The whole British system must be stamped out.

Thus, the summit between President Trump and Chinese President Xi Jinping was intended to provide the basis for a close relationship between these two major countries to be able to resolve their differences and to work together for the advancement of humanity. Instead, the discussions took place under conditions of escalating crisis. The Chinese delegation must have been totally taken aback by this major military operation in the midst of such an important meeting. However, after President Trump informed President Xi about the bombing, following the state dinner on the evening of April 6, meetings continued with the Chinese delegation the next morning as scheduled, and were concluded by early afternoon.

The personal chemistry between the two leaders was good. They had already established a positive rapport previously through their mutual correspondence and their phone calls. There were many smiling faces during the pauses with the press during the breaks in the more serious discussions. President Trump said that the two leaders had developed an "outstanding" relationship and that "lots of very potentially bad problems will be going away." President Xi also was quite pleased with the reception his delegation—which included four Politburo members—had been given by the President. The summit, he said "held a uniquely important significance for the Sino-U.S. relationship."

"President Trump made excellent preparation for our country's representatives and gave us a warm reception," Xi said. "We recently have had in-depth and lengthy communications to this end, and arrived at many common understandings, the most important being deepening our friendship and building a kind of trust in keeping with the Sino-U.S. working relationship and friendship."

President Trump also had most of his cabinet with him at the summit, including Secretary of State Rex Tillerson, Treasury Secretary Stephen Mnuchin, and Commerce Secretary Wilbur Ross. President Xi also extended an invitation to President Trump to visit China this year, which President Trump readily accepted. President Xi also invited the U.S. President to join the Belt and Road Initiative.

The two presidents also established a new and cabinet-level framework for negotiations, the United States-China Comprehensive Dialogue, which will be overseen by them. This mechanism will replace the previous U.S.-China Strategic and Economic Dialogue, which was criticized by the Trump people as being a "talk-shop" with no practical results. With the new format, they hope to realize concrete results within a short period. The Dialogue will have four pillars:

- The Diplomatic and Security Dialogue,
- The Comprehensive Economic Dialogue,
- The Law Enforcement and Cyber-security Dialogue, and
- The Social and Cultural Issues Dialogue.

The two presidents had discussed the important issues of trade, and have decided to develop a one-hundred-day action plan on U.S.-China trade which will have "way-stations of accomplishment along the way," according to Treasury Secretary Steven Mnuchin.

There was also a discussion regarding investment and eliminating the obstacles that remain in achieving a genuine bilateral investment treaty between the two countries. Secretary Tillerson also indicated that there had been a longer discussion on the North Korean nuclear program, with a renewed commitment by both sides to denuclearize the Korean peninsula and have increased cooperation in convincing the North Koreans to give up their program, although there was no "package arrangement" on the topic, he said. Tillerson said that President Xi shared the U.S. view that this situation has reached a very serious stage.

While on the surface, the summit seemed to have achieved the limited goals it had set: to establish a good working relationship between the leaders and to conduct a thorough discussion of the issues on which the two countries were divided, the escalating crisis provoked by the U.S. attack on Syria still remains.

Some Chinese analysts have already expressed the suspicion that the operation was timed to underline the determination of the United States to use military action, if necessary, against the Democratic People's Republic of Korea (DPRK), if the nuclear threat remains, thereby putting pressure on China to take a harder line against its North Korean neighbor, although no one should be so foolish as to think that conducting any kind of military strike against the DPRK, in contrast to Syria, could be done without immediate retaliation from North Korea. The unilateral exertion of U.S. power in the Middle East also sent the subtle message that the "major power relationship" sought by China, a relationship of equality, was still a distant goal.

The response of the Chinese Foreign Ministry to the Syrian strike was unusually muted. Chinese Foreign Ministry spokeswoman Hua Chunying, on April 8, reiterated that China opposes the use of chemical weapons "by any country, organization, or person for any purpose and under any circumstance." At the same time, she said that the matter deserved a thorough UN investigation in order to really determine who was responsible "and on the basis of solid evidence, reaching a conclusion which can stand the test of history and facts."

At the moment, President Trump is headed straight for a major war, despite his own inclinations and his promises to the voters.

Lyndon LaRouche has called for an immediate crisis summit of President Trump with Russia's President Putin, to avert war while there is still time. The British system must be ended.

Helga Zepp-LaRouche Speaks to Sputnik Ahead of Xi-Trump Summit

April 5—The following is an edited transcript of an interview by Sputnik with Helga Zepp-LaRouche, regarding the April 6-April 7 summit between Presidents Xi Jinping and Donald Trump: The interview was conducted before the summit.

Sputnik: What will the tone of the meeting be?

Helga Zepp-LaRouche: Oh, I think it will be actually cordial. The Western media, who are usually wrong, are trying to reduce this whole question to some geopolitical conflict, but I think both sides have prepared this meeting very well. I think, when Secretary of State Tillerson was in Beijing last month to prepare the visit, he said that the U.S.-China relationship in the Trump Administration would be a very positive relationship, built on no confrontation, no conflict, mutual respect, and always searching for a "win-win" solution. And that was exactly the formulation that was used by Xi Jinping in 2012 when he called for building a new type of major-country relationship between China and the United States.

Michael Vadon
Donald Trump, 2015

Now, this was rejected by President Obama at the time. But the fact that Tillerson is now using the exact same formulations shows a very positive signal. And I think that since China has put the New Silk Road policy on the table—or the Belt and Road Initiative, as it's called now—since 2013, and has been building this New Silk Road, with the idea that the United States should join it, too, I would not be surprised at all, if something like that would be discussed, to the big surprise of many.

Sputnik: I see. Now, earlier Trump had accused China of raping the U.S. economy. He called the country a currency manipulator, and even threatened to impose high tariffs on Chinese imports. With that said, what reaction should we expect from the Chinese leader? What positions will they be taking?

Zepp-LaRouche: I don't think that Xi Jinping will react to the campaign tone of the *candidate* Trump, because now Trump is President. And I think if they put on the table the idea that China would invest in the infrastructure in the United States, Trump himself has announced the need to have a $1 trillion program to reconstruct the American infrastructure. There

flickr/Narendra Modi
Xi Jinping, 2016

was recently a conference in Hong Kong where Chinese economists estimated that the real requirement [for the United States] is $8 trillion. Now, the way to reduce the trade-deficit is by direct Chinese investment in infrastructure, maybe not immediately, but indirectly; maybe one would have an infrastructure bank, where China could put its investments, or some solution like that.

But I'm convinced that they will absolutely come out of this summit with results beneficial to both countries.

Sputnik: It's interesting that you talk about a positive solution to the trade-deficit, that you just mentioned, where China could possibly create a special investment bank; but is there anything else that Trump could do to somehow reduce this trade-deficit? Or is there any way that President Trump could somehow improve the relations between the countries, and improve the trade between the countries?

Zepp-LaRouche: Well, Trump has recently mentioned several times that he wants to go back to the American System of economy, the system of Alexander Hamilton, of Lincoln, of Henry Clay; and it is actually that system which made the United States great following the War of Independence. And that was a highly protectionist system. Alexander Hamilton created the United States by creating a National Bank, a credit system; and for example, the German economist Friedrich List pointed to the difference between the American System of economy and the British System of economy, meaning that the American System which was created by Hamilton basically says the only source of wealth is the creativity and productivity of the labor force, as compared to the British System which says you have to buy cheap and sell expensive, and control trade, and keep labor costs as low as possible.

So, if you actually look at what China has been doing with the Chinese economic miracle of the last thirty years, it is much closer to the philosophy of Alexander Hamilton, than it would be to the system of globalization and so-called "free trade." I think that the Chinese system of free trade is not exactly the same one as what the British and the Americans under the Obama and Bush administrations have been thinking about.

So, if Trump says, "OK, globalization led to an outsourcing of productive jobs, and I want to recreate the American economy," well, that "recreation of the American economy" is exactly how to reduce the trade deficit, because the reason why there's a deficit is that many American products in the last sixteen years of the Bush and Obama administration became increasingly less competitive, for example the car industry. The reason why you have more cars imported, from Japan, Korea, Germany, than the other way around, is that these cars are better than American cars.

And what America has to do, what President Trump has to do—and I think that's what he intends to do—is to reconstruct the American economy on the highest productive level. The infrastructure is only the precondition, but then there will be other areas, like in nuclear fission, but especially the development of fusion technology, Space cooperation with other countries. So

there are many areas where you can leapfrog into the most productive areas in the economy, and I think that's what Trump intends to do.

Sputnik: It's interesting that you talk about that, and I really like that you mention that subject. Unfortunately we'll have to do that at a different time.

Apart from the issue that we've already discussed, are there any other issues that will be on the table between the Chinese leader and the U.S. President?

Zepp-LaRouche: Well, obviously, the North Korea issue will be very high up on the agenda, given the recent missile tests by North Korea. But there, one has to understand that North Korea is doing this, not because they intend an aggression against South Korea or Japan, or the United States. They are doing it in reaction to the deployment of the THAAD missiles, which both China and Russia have also said are security threats to their own national security, and North Korea is reacting to the very big maneuvers involving the United States, Japan, and South Korea, which are going on right now.

So the way to reduce that, and it would be my guess, is that they will get an agreement to re-propose the Six-Party talks, to try to find a solution, or even have maybe Five-Party talks, to try to really work out a real solution one could offer to North Korea. But it is my conviction that the only way this conflict can be solved forever, is to extend the New Silk Road into Korea, have a unification of South and North Korea, and then develop them together, with the sovereignty of North Korea being taken into account. But I think the way to overcome the terrible economic hardships is also by using the high-skilled labor you have in North Korea! People don't know that there is actually a highly developed labor force in North Korea.

So I think the New Silk Road/Belt and Road Initiative, even in the short or medium term, would be the framework with which to solve the North Korea problem forever.

Sputnik: All right. Well, on that note, I would like to thank you very much for joining me today, Helga. It was a pleasure having you here, and I'd love to have you back in the future.

Zepp-LaRouche: OK, thank you.

III. Southwest Asia and Africa

A MARSHALL PLAN FOR SOUTHWEST ASIA

Crossroads of the Continents

by Hussein Askary

April 10—This text is an updated version of Part 6 of the Arabic translation of the EIR Special Report, The New Silk Road Becomes the World Land-Bridge, which was published in February 2016. Part 6 of the Arabic version also included an appendix on the reconstruction of Syria, separately published in *EIR* Dec. 23, 2016: *Aleppo Will Rise from the Ashes of War*.

The visit by Chinese President Xi Jinping in January 2016 to Saudi Arabia, Egypt, and Iran should be seen as an economic and strategic turning point in the history of the Southwest Asia region. The visit has to be used as far as possible to build the foundation for a new modus operandi of peace through economic development. This, obviously, has to go hand in hand with resolving the crisis in Syria politically and the eradication of terrorism militarily as necessary. This visit, in which President Xi invited these nations to join the Economic Belt of the New Silk Road, came at one of the darkest moments in this region where three wars are raging simultaneously, in Syria, Iraq, and Yemen, and many other nations, such as Egypt, Libya Turkey, Lebanon, Kuwait, and Saudi Arabia, are targeted by terrorist activities. President Xi's visit also came one week after the Chinese Foreign Ministry issued the first ever Chinese political paper concerning the Arab world, focusing on the necessity of economic cooperation and building the basic infrastructure projects along the New Silk Road, and promoting nuclear power and industrial development as the key elements to stabilize and resolve the crises in the region. This visit and the economic,

cultural, and trade agreements that were signed between China and the three countries President Xi visited created an atmosphere of optimism and openness toward the idea of the New Silk Road.

This Chinese initiative, if the countries of the region pursue its content and principles, would realize the ideas and initiatives promoted by EIR and the Schiller Institute for this region over more than 30 years.

In a speech delivered at the Zayed Center in Abu Dhabi in June 2002, Lyndon LaRouche presented the economic perspective for the Gulf nations, being "on the cross-roads" of the Eurasia-Africa continents. Indeed, the geographical location of Southwest Asia nations on the most vital trade and transport routes between three continents gives them a unique advantage. If these nations were to integrate and transform their

EIRNS

Lyndon LaRouche with Dr. Ubaid bin Masood al-Jahni between sessions of the conference on "The Role of Oil and Gas in World Politics" at the Zayed Centre in Abu Dhabi in June 2002, where he was a featured speaker.

economies to facilitate the future economic development of the Eurasian landmass and Africa, they will play a key role in these developments, ensuring at the same time their long-term economic, political, and cultural survival beyond the era of fossil fuels. This region is immediately important for economic development in other parts of the world, especially East Asia, because of its oil and gas resource base. For example, 48% of the world's crude oil exports originate from this region, and 80-90% of that oil goes to the Asian nations of China, India, Japan, and South Korea. Almost two-thirds of the oil and natural gas reserves of the world are located in this region and proximately adjacent areas in North Africa and Central Asia. Thus, this region is a choke-point for the supply of energy. Although still dominated by Anglo-American geopolitics, with an anti-imperialist policy this region could become a bridge for peace and development.

The two best examples in the region of the tendency toward the new paradigm of development of the physical economy represented by the BRICS nations (Brazil, Russia, India, China, South Africa) are Egypt and Iran. Since the second revolution in June 2013, and the election of President Abdulfattah el-Sisi, Egypt has taken steps to move away from its crisis-ridden and dependent status to become a truly developing nation. And that despite massive economic and social ills that have accumulated over many decades, and in the face of a terrible assault on the nation by the terrorist group the Islamic State (IS). The new tendency is exemplified by Egypt's efforts to utilize as much as possible its national resources, financial and human, that have been idle for many years. These resources are now channeled into a comprehensive and well-planned national development strategy based on mega projects put on schedules for super-accelerated completion, as was achieved in the digging of the second Suez Canal in a record time of one year (completed in November 2015). There is also a renewed focus on industrial development and reclaiming the desert for agricultural and urban development to rebalance the demographic discrepancy in the country.

Egypt has also benefitted from the Chinese policy which regards Egypt as a key strategic transport and logistic hub on the Maritime Silk Road between Asia and Europe. In addition, President el-Sisi has established a very special political and strategic relationship

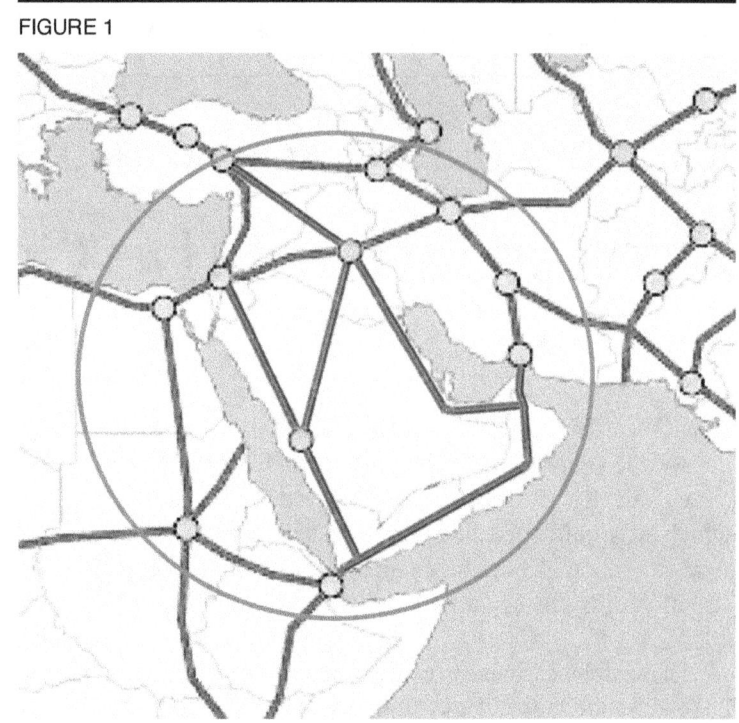

FIGURE 1

with Russia President Vladimir Putin, and economic cooperation has been progressing between the two countries, including the signing of an agreement to build Egypt's first commercial nuclear power plant in El-Dhaba on the Mediterranean coast. (Being geographically part of Africa, Egypt's role is dealt with in Part 10 of the EIR Special Report.)

The second important example is Iran. Although this part of the report is focused on Iran's role as a key connection between Asia and the region and Europe, it is strategically very important to normalize Iran's relations to the Arab states in the region in general and Egypt in particular in order to thwart the attempts to drive the region into an unprecedented religious and sectarian war that can lead to the fragmentation and destruction of almost all large nations in the entire region.

In addition, the natural physical-economic geographical area includes Iran, Turkey, Syria, Egypt, Sudan, Ethiopia, Djibouti, and the Gulf Cooperation Council (GCC) countries [see **Figure 1**]. This region is not only the greatest source of petroleum resources in the world, containing more than two-thirds of all known reserves of oil and gas in the world, but also a natural bridge between the continents, a center of many ancient civilizations, and home to about 450 million people, most of whom are under the age of 30 with a relatively good education. This population is expected to double in the coming 30-50 years. In addition, it contains massive non-fuel mineral resources, and even large water resources if used wisely and effectively. It is potentially one of the largest markets for industrial and high-technology goods, from which it has been locked out for several decades and now is hungry for these necessary products for its development. The region as a whole does not lack financial resources, with more than $1 trillion just in the Sovereign Wealth Funds of the GCC countries alone.

Broader Development Potential in Southwest Asia

There is a very paradoxical situation in this region when it comes to the correlation of living standards, culture, education, and economic and financial wealth. Since the oil crisis of 1973 in particular, these countries have been divided into two categories, the so-called rich ones and the poor cousins. The rich ones are the oil exporting countries in the Gulf, members of the GCC, which have small populations and large mineral wealth. They are also members of the British imperial club, and are coddled by the United States and Europe. The others have fewer resources and larger populations, and have been cursed by the British and the United States. The poorer ones include Iran, Iraq, Syria, Lebanon, the Palestinian people, and Egypt. Jordan has vacillated between these two camps politically, but economically is one of the poorest in the region. The paradox here is that the population in the seemingly poorer countries has much higher levels of education, more advanced labor skills, and a deeper sense of historical identity. The richer ones are living in a strange dichotomy between material wealth and primitive traditions and religious extremism. Technological progress is welcome, but only as a pragmatic power tool, not for the improvement of the cultural and physical conditions of the citizens of the states or their future missions. An educated middle class is obviously a political threat to the ruling families. The discrepancy between the small native labor force and the foreign workers (constituting 80-90% of the labor force in the private sector in most of the richer countries) threatens to pose serious problems in the near future, as mass unemployment among the natives increases, and the lack of basic labor rights among guest workers become more tangible as their wages do not match the real increase in prices globally. Obviously it is difficult to sustain a society of half slaves.

In the poorer group of nations, a great number of the best brains and educated persons have fled these countries due to civil wars, political oppression, and wars or invasions by foreign armies such as in the case of Iraq or foreign-backed terrorist groups as in the case of Syria today. Economic sanctions against Iraq, Iran, and Syria, and International Monetary Fund (IMF)/World Bank policies imposed on Egypt, have led to the deterioration of living standards, infrastructure, and educational systems. All this has set back the development of these nations many decades. Yemen has suffered all three— IMF conditionalities, terrorism, and recently a foreign campaign of intensive bombardment and economic blockade.

The Schiller Institute program for the development of the region, now possible with the New Silk Road Initiative, will shift this imbalance dramatically because the financial and mineral wealth, human resources, and skills will be directed toward one unified mission for all the countries—national and regional integrated development. Youth among the native populations will be trained, allowing them to join the labor force to build their nations and green the desert, in similar fashion as the Franklin Roosevelt era (1933) New Deal and associated Civilian Conservation Corps (CCC) programs during the Great Depression pulled unemployed people in America off the streets into the national reconstruction projects, helping turn the United States into the most powerful economic nation on earth during World War II. The brain drain will be stopped, and hundreds of thousands of scientists and well-educated people working in exile or as expatriates in Europe and the Americas will feel safe to come home and serve their nations. The financial and mineral wealth and whatever national credit that can be generated in the rich countries, can be matched up with the skills of the labor of the others in the short term to launch the reconstruction process. A common credit system established through a development bank can fill the credit gaps among the oil-poor or water-poor countries.

The GCC region boasts of the largest Sovereign Wealth Funds (SWF) in the world, with a total of $1.5 trillion. Most of that oil wealth is not invested in the region but in financial and real estate markets in mainly Britain and the United States. The author proposes the establishment of an "Arab Infrastructure Development Bank" with a capital of at least $100 billion.

Nations such as Yemen and Jordan would no longer be left at the mercy of the IMF just because they cannot pull together their credit potentials to launch an economic development process. A nation such as Jordan will be aided to build its first nuclear power plants, and will upgrade its human potential and processing of natural resources (such as phosphate and uranium) and become a rich nation within one generation, rather than waiting desperately for hand-outs from the United States, European Union (EU), or IMF and World Bank. Sharing know-how, for example in dealing with desert conditions, agricultural problems will be dealt with most effectively through establishing a unified scientific research center functioning under a common executive authority. Right now, due to the policies of fomenting religious strife and wars throughout the region all the way to the Caucasus and western China, the entire region is threatened by 30-year religious/sectarian war from which it might never recover. This vicious cycle must be broken. There are global preconditions, of course, such as shifting the murderous geopolitical system of divide and conquer of the British Empire, that are required to assist these nations to shift focus from destruction to construction. The integration of this region into the Eurasian-African Land-Bridge will be key, and will benefit the world and these nations.

The Bridge Among Continents

Many links integrating the region into the Eurasian-African Land-Bridge are already underway [**Figure 2**]. The inauguration of the Mashhad-Sarakhs (Turkmenistan) railway in 1996 by then-President Hashemi Rafsanjani connected Iran to China and further revived the ancient Silk Road. Two years later, Iran completed its connection to the northwest, to Turkey, reviving the Silk Road connection to Europe. In 2001, the Mashhad-Bafq-Bandar Abbas line was completed, connecting landlocked Central Asia to the Persian Gulf. Iran also completed the Bafq-Kerman-Zahedan railway to Paki-

FIGURE 2

Map of UIC Middle East Railways

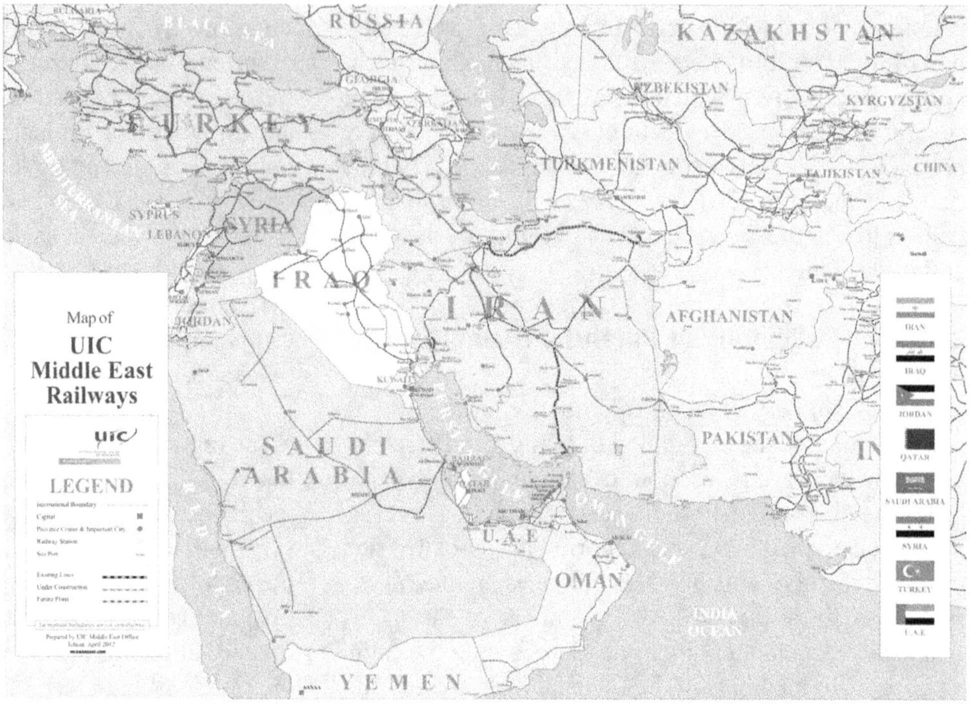

International Union of Railways, April 2012

stan, connecting Iran to the Indian subcontinent. There is also the strategic continental International North-South Corridor, which goes from Russia to India. There is an agreement among Russia, Iran, and India to build a trade route through the Caucasus and Central Asia, through the Iranian railway network. This will tie in the port of Chabahar in southern Iran on the Gulf of Oman, on which development work is commencing. India is very interested in this, because shipping by sea takes about three weeks to the Black Sea, while the railway system through Russia takes one week.

Iran is connecting its south-north railway network to Russia via the Caucasus region through both Azerbaijan and Armenia in cooperation with Russia. On March 3, the first train crossed the bridge built over the Astaracay River, which forms the border between Iran and Azerbaijan. The railway between Astra in Azerbaijan and Rasht in Iran is the last missing piece in the International South-North Transport Corridor. In January 2013, the Armenian Ministry of Transport and Communication, Dubai-based investment company Rasia, and Russian Railways (RZD) subsidiary South Caucasus Railway (SCR) signed a trilateral agreement for the construction of the Southern Armenia Railway. The agreement covers the construction of a 316 km railway linking Gavar, 50 km east of Yerevan near Lake Sevar, with the Iranian border near Meghri. The electrified, single-track railway line will be part of a new north-south corridor linking the Black Sea and the Persian Gulf, according to Armenian authorities. Interestingly, China is also involved in the project because the feasibility studies conducted by Rasia selected China Communications Construction Company to become the lead member of a consortium that will be responsible for the project. The Iranian section of the project is under construction, but the Armenian part is stalled due to tensions with Azerbaijan, through which territory part of this line has to pass on the way to the Iranian border.

The Iran-Pakistan gas pipeline, a vital economic endeavor for Pakistan's energy security and prosperity that was pursued by the Pakistani government despite American pressure, is crucial to bring Pakistan on board a regional solution for the situation in Afghanistan. The Iranian part of the pipeline was completed earlier. On March 11, 2013, construction work on the Pakistani section of the pipeline was inaugurated by President of Pakistan Asif Ali Zardari and President of Iran Mahmoud Ahmadinejad. The pipeline in Pakistan had been expected to be constructed in 22 months with the participation and financial backing of Iran, but construction of the Pakistani section of the pipeline was suspended due to pressure from the United States. Obama Administration and Saudi Arabia. As part of that pressure, and due its desperate need for gas, Pakistan was forced to sign an agreement with Qatar for the purchase of an 1.3 million tons annually of liquified natural gas (LNG) for 20 years. The gas will be delivered by tanker to the port of Gwadar, and will cost Pakistan approximately $15 billion. Internal economic and political instability in Pakistan, in addition to pressure from the Saudi-British-American axis to isolate Iran, is a major obstacle to Iran-Pakistan cooperation. But building a modern Afghan nation will require modern institutions and a prosperous and thriving economy.

China, India, and Iran are already the three largest economic partners of Afghanistan. The country has the potential of soon standing on its own economic feet, as it will be enabled to explore and exploit the massive mineral resources in its soil. These resources are estimated to make Afghanistan a world-class mining nation.

Completing the bridge to the west, Iran also has been active in promoting trade, transport, and economic exchange with Turkey and Iraq. In addition to a gas pipeline and railway to Turkey, Iran has been building a gas pipeline to Iraq, to be extended farther to Syria and the Mediterranean. A railway is planned to run adjacent to the pipeline and road projects. However, the destabilization of Syria and Iraq through sectarian violence has halted work on the projects. Thus, Iran will continue to be a key element of the New Silk Road or Eurasian Land-Bridge. Turkey is also a key player in connecting Asia to Eastern Europe across the Bosphorus—new bridges and tunnels have been built and others are under construction to connect the Asian and European sides of Turkey at the capital, Istanbul.

Extending the Iran-Turkish Connection to Europe

Rebuilding the Hijaz Railway from Turkey through Syria, Jordan, and Saudi Arabia to Eden in Yemen was under consideration before the events in Syria broke out in the Spring of 2011. From Yemen, a tunnel or bridge to Djibouti on the Horn of Africa was also being considered at the time by the Yemeni government and corporations from the United Arab Emirates (UAE). From Yemen, through Oman and the UAE, a tunnel to the Iranian port of Bandar Abbas across the Hormuz Strait is a feasible transport corridor that would connect Asia to Africa directly. A railway and highway connection northward from the UAE through Saudi Arabia, Qatar, Bahrain, and Kuwait that will potentially connect to Iraq and Turkey, and through Syria to the Mediterranean, is under consideration by the GCC nations. From Jordan and northern Saudi Arabia, a bridge/causeway across the southern end of the Gulf of Aqaba to connect to Egypt was under study by the government of former President Hosni Mubarak in 2009. Almost all these projects are shelved now due to the political and military destabilization of the region. Israel's connection to these networks, including gas and electricity networks, was openly discussed in the 1990s, but has been excluded since the collapse of the peace process between the right-wing Israeli government under Benjamin Netanyahu and the Palestinian Authority. All these projects, nonetheless, can be put back on the fast track, whenever a just international political order is established.

The Proposed Inter-Arab State Transport Projects

The Schiller Institute priority list of projects to integrate the Arab countries by railway and roads includes:

• **The Berlin-Baghdad Railway and extensions:**

FIGURE 3

MAJOR DESERTS

The vast desert that stretches almost continuously from the Atlantic coast of North Africa through the Arabian Peninsula, all the way through to western China, represents a major challenge for economic development for all the nations involved.

A Common Enemy: The Desert

What is striking about transcontinental regions where the Silk Road passes is that the landscape is a vast desert stretching almost continuously from the Atlantic coast of North Africa through the Arabian Peninsula, across the Zagros Mountains to Iran and Central Asia, and all the way to western China [**Figure 3**]. The size of that transcontinental stretch of desert is about 13 million square kilometers. Areas that receive between 250 and 500 mm of annual rainfall are usually deemed to be semi-desert or semi-arid. In general, large parts of the area receive an average annual rainfall of 250 mm or less. Many parts of the great deserts get less than that, and sometimes no rainfall at all.

The major deserts of the world are located within these regions. These deserts are currently expanding, due to not only the lack of adequate economic and sociopolitical measures, but also the destruction of existing green areas through the mismanagement of local resources. Long cycles of drought have also contributed to the expansion of the desert. Sandstorms and dust storms are frequent events in Southwest Asia, especially in the Gulf region, but even extending to Iran, Afghanistan, Pakistan, and India. While sandstorms rise up to tens of meters, dust storms can rise to several kilometers into space. And they can cover whole countries. Their impact on urban areas can shut down airports, ports, hospitals, schools, and other vital facilities.

Attacking the Desert from the Fertile Crescent: The area stretching from Lebanon to Syria and down Mesopotamia to the Gulf is called the Fertile Crescent. Historians claim that agriculture in the world started in this region. However, it is not so fertile any more. By better managing the natural resources and creating new resources of land and water, green belts, and trees; improving vegetation selection; and applying advanced agronomy and animal husbandry and especially space-era science and capabilities, a new array of productive activity can be established where once was desert.

In the 1970s and 1980s, "green belts" were being planned for eastern Syria, western Iraq, and parts of eastern Jordan. With successive rows of forests, the ex-

Istanbul-Mosul-Baghdad-Basra-Kuwait-Dhahran-Doha-Abu Dhabi-Musqat-Salalah (Oman).

• **The Hijaz Railway and extensions:** Istanbul-Aleppo-Damascus (Beirut)-Amman-Jeddah-Mecca-Alhudaidah (Yemen)-Aden.

• **The Orient Express and extensions:** Istanbul-Tripoli (Lebanon)-Beirut-West Bank-Gaza-Sinai-Alexandria. An extension from Tehran through Baghdad to Palmyra in Syria, Damascus, Beirut, and Latakia will connect Central Asia and the Persian Gulf to the eastern Mediterranean coast.

• **Zubaida Road (Road of Pilgrims):** Baghdad-Najaf-Alhail-Almadina-Mecca and further to Yemen.

• **The Nile Line/Alexandria-Cape Town:** Alexandria-Cairo-Aswan-Khartoum-Addis Abeba-Djibouti and further into the Great Lakes regions and East Africa to South Africa.

• **The Maghreb Road:** Alexandria-Tripoli (Libya)-Tunis-Alger-Wajdah-Fez-Tanger-Casablanca.

A special connection between the Arabian Peninsula and Sinai and Africa is being seriously considered by the governments of Egypt and Saudi Arabia, including a bridge/causeway or tunnel across the Tiran Strait in the south of the Gulf of Aqaba.

Parallel to these high-speed transport corridors, a joint network for transportation and transfer of electricity, oil, gas, and water has to be established to open new areas that are generally desert today for development.

FIGURE 4

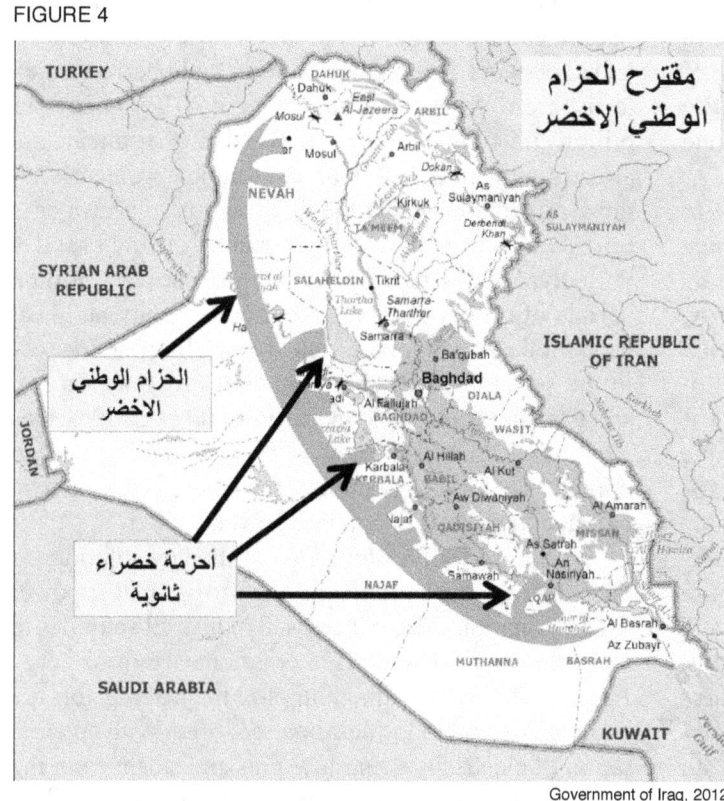

مقترح الحزام
الوطني الاخضر

الحزام الوطني
الاخضر

أحزمة خضراء
ثانوية

Government of Iraq, 2012

FIGURE 5

EIRNS, 2012

The Southeastern Anatolian Project, called the GAP, would dam the Tigris and Euphrates rivers in Turkey, and create a huge reservoir behind the Ataturk Dam.

pansion of desert areas can be stopped and gradually reclaimed. In Iraq, for example, a plan was prepared decades ago to create a green belt in the west of the country [**Figure 4**].

Due to the series of geopolitical wars and destruction of Iraq's infrastructure and agriculture, these plans were never implemented. Furthermore, the degradation of the soil and land has expanded the arid areas. There now are active operations, although limited in scope, to return to this idea. Iraq and Iran signed an agreement in 2010 to invest approximately $2.1 billion in projects to create green belts in the southwestern part of Iraq, especially in the region of the cities of Karbala and Najaf, which are frequently hit by sand and dust storms. One project, for example, established a 27-kilometer-long crescent lined with thousands of newly planted trees in a belt 100-200 meters wide. It is irrigated by 50 shallow wells (35 to 50 meters deep). The area is now the front line of Karbala's battle against increasingly frequent sandstorms and salinity and erosion of the soil. The project has involved planting more than 100,000 olive, palm, eucalyptus, and other trees, all of which were chosen for their resistance to heat and soil salinity.

Water Sources: The obvious question is, of course: Where will all the water come from to back this massive war on the desert? The region is dominated by two major water systems—the Tigris and Euphrates rivers basin, and the Jordan River basin. The latter is a relatively limited water system dominated by military and political conflicts for the control of the water between Israel and Lebanon, Syria, and Jordan. The Mesopotamian water system is larger and has greater potential.

The general problem in this and other desert regions is that a great part of the rainfall disappears due to evaporation, transpiration, and run-off. To collect and use as much as possible of the precipitation, large-scale water infrastructure systems are required. One of the most ambitious water infrastructure projects in the region, the South Eastern Anatolian Project (in Turkish abbreviation GAP) [**Figure 5**], has been under way during the past two decades. However, this project has created major problems for the countries downstream, Syria and Iraq, because it blocks the natural flow of the Tigris and Euphrates. What is needed is to establish a scheme of cooperation among the three countries, and even Iran, which shares some of the tributaries of the Tigris with Iraq, to make the entire Mesopotamian basin function most effectively as one unit.

Legal and technical agreements have to be made to ensure the sound management of the system and a just share in the water. The GAP, begun more than 20 years ago and modeled on the Tennessee Valley Authority, envisions 22 dams to provide 7.4 GW of electricity, water management, irrigation, and flood control. Located in southeastern Turkey, the project covers 10% of the country's land area—75,000 square km and nine provinces in the Euphrates-Tigris basins and southeastern plains—and accounts for 20% of Turkey's arable land. The project includes the development of infrastructure of all types required for integrating the entire region, including transportation, power, tunnels, and canals. According to Turkish government estimates, when the projects are completed, 1.7 million hectares of land will be effectively irrigated. The region represents 28% of Turkey's total hydraulic potential, with the Ataturk Dam at its center.

There is a large number of dams in Syria and Iraq, but more can be done, especially in northern Iran, to build dams on the tributaries of the Tigris River that flow inside the Iraqi Zagros Mountains, such as the Greater Zab. Building new and maintaining the existing relatively modern system of dams, barrages, and canals in Syria and Iraq will rescue these two countries from flooding during the Spring and drought during the Summer.

Seawater Desalination: One thing that has become clear for the governments of the Gulf and other dry regions throughout the world is that the best solution to secure water for drinking, other urban usage, and industry is the desalination of sea water. Steps have been taken by the countries in the region to build conventional desalination plants on a large scale, investing heavily in the combined water desalination/power generation process with the use of fossil fuels such as natural gas and oil. More than two-thirds of the world's production of fresh water by desalination occurs in the region. Saudi Arabia alone produces 25 million cubic meters of water per day, which is estimated to be one-half of the world's total.

The U.A.E. produces around 3 million cubic meters per day. However, these countries will have to more

than double that amount of desalinated water in the next decade and triple it in the decade beyond to meet projected demand. Water consumption had been expected to rise from 8 billion cubic meters in 2012 to about 11 billion cubic meters in 2016. Massive investments are already projected in this area. A major problem with these projections is that the desalination of seawater is reliant on thermal power plants run by oil and gas. Reportedly, Saudi Arabia, for example, uses 1.5 million barrels of oil daily to produce the electricity and heat used for desalination. It is a net physical economic loss in the sense that valuable industrial raw material (oil and gas) that could yield many times its value if used as a base for petrochemical and other products is instead burned to achieve a relatively low energy-flux-density output compared with nuclear power.

Nuclear Desalination: One of the key solutions to this water shortage problem is the use of nuclear power for desalination and for increased industrial activities in the petrochemical field. As International Atomic Energy Agency studies show, medium-size nuclear reactors are especially suitable for desalination, often with cogeneration of electricity using low-pressure steam from the turbine and hot seawater feed from the final cooling system.

There are many new technologies being tested in this field, all of which point in the direction of higher temperature and pressure, something that can only be achieved efficiently through nuclear power. Fourth generation high-temperature nuclear power plants have long been proven as the most efficient, but almost no effort is being taken to invest in them. At the moment, Iran is the only country in the region that has an operating large civilian nuclear power plant. The Bushehr plant, a product of cooperation between Iran and Russia, was inaugurated officially in September 2011, and reached its full power production capacity (1,000 MW) in August 2012. Iran is planning to build several new nuclear reactors, with the expressed aim of increasing the energy output of the country and desalinating seawater. In December 2006, the GCC announced that the Council was commissioning a study on the peaceful use of nuclear energy. In 2007, the member states signed an agreement with the IAEA to cooperate on a feasibility study for a regional nuclear power and desalination program. The U.A.E. was the first of the countries in the study to launch its nuclear power program. The Emirates Nuclear Energy Corporation (ENEC) was established in 2009 in Abu Dhabi as an investment vehicle

FIGURE 6
Features of the Oasis Plan, 1980

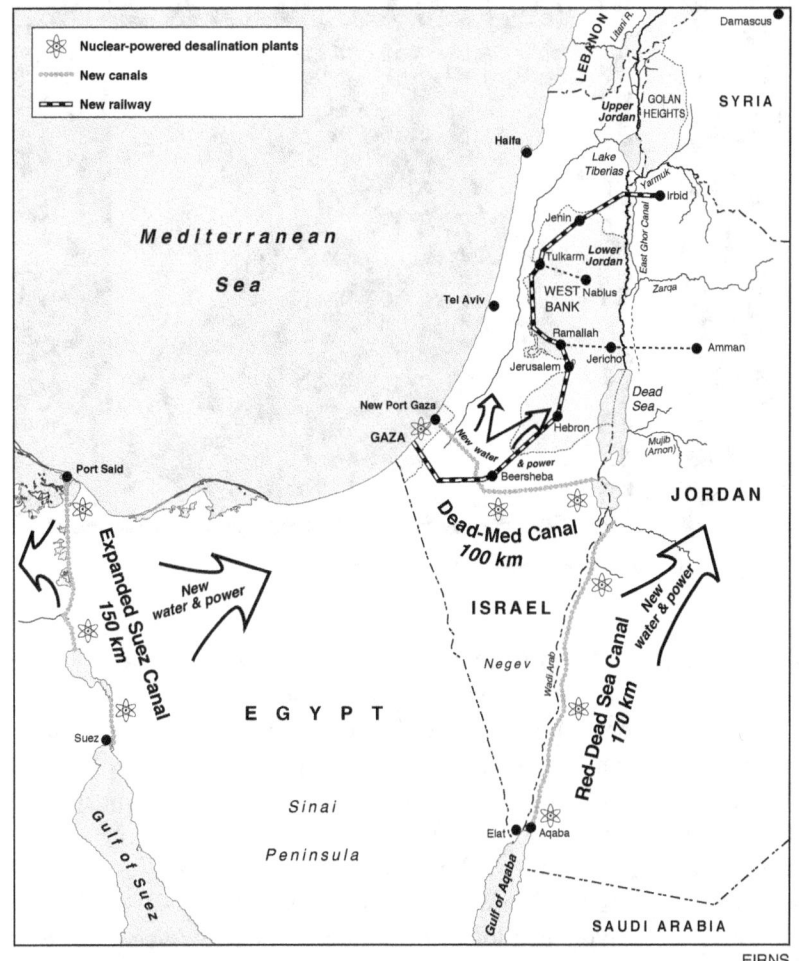

EIRNS

The roots of this plan for solving the water crisis in the Middle East go back to the mid-1970s, but it was codified in 1990, when LaRouche was campaigning to stop the first Gulf War.

geopolitical reasons. In 2013 Jordan signed an agreement with Russia to build the first nuclear power plant in the country. The expressed purpose of the project was water desalination. Israel has similar plans for nuclear power development for desalination purposes.

Lyndon LaRouche has argued since the 1970s that without turning to nuclear power to secure energy and water in this region, as prescribed in his Oasis Plan [**Figure 6**], no peace process can endure under the economic pressures including the shortage of water and power in the region. The Palestinian people especially, who have been deprived of even the little existing underground water by Israel, will have no chance of survival without large-scale seawater desalination. A United Nations report issued in 2012 determined that the Gaza Strip would be "unlivable by 2020" due to the complete depletion and contamination of the ground water aquifers. Lebanon and the coastal cities of Syria are experiencing the same water crisis as the Palestinian areas. Only a combination of modern water management systems and nuclear desalination can reverse the catastrophic conditions in these two countries.

Groundwater: Space technology is now being used to discover and manage groundwater. A major breakthrough in the exploration of groundwater, using space technologies of remote sensing in combination with geological and hydrological innovations, was achieved in the past few years by the French company Radar Technologies International (RTI). Geologist Dr. Alain Gachet, founder and president of RTI, developed the patented WATEX technology, an algorithm that transforms Space Shuttle radar images of Earth and other remote sensing tools into images for mapping groundwater moisture and discovering groundwater aquifers with amazing precision.

Applying WATEX in the refugee camps in Darfur in 2004 contributed to the exploration of 1,000 productive wells, and literally saved the lives of hundreds of thousands of refugees stranded in the desert in Chad and Sudan. In 2013, application of WATEX in the dry region of Turkana in northwest Kenya achieved even greater

for the nuclear program. In December 2009, ENEC announced its acceptance of the bid offered by the South Korean Korea Electric Power Corporation (Kepco) to build four 1,400 MW nuclear plants by 2020 at the cost of $20 billion. The construction of the first of the four plants was started in Baraka in July 2012, and the fourth and last will be completed in 2020.

Saudi Arabia announced through the royal decree of King Abdullah bin Abdul-Aziz Al-Saud in April 2010 the establishment of the King Abdullah City for Atomic and Renewable Energy. Shortly after that, the Saudi government announced plans to build 16 nuclear power reactors by 2030. Unlike the Iranian nuclear program, the GCC's programs are welcomed and approved by the United States and the West generally, for obvious

FIGURE 7

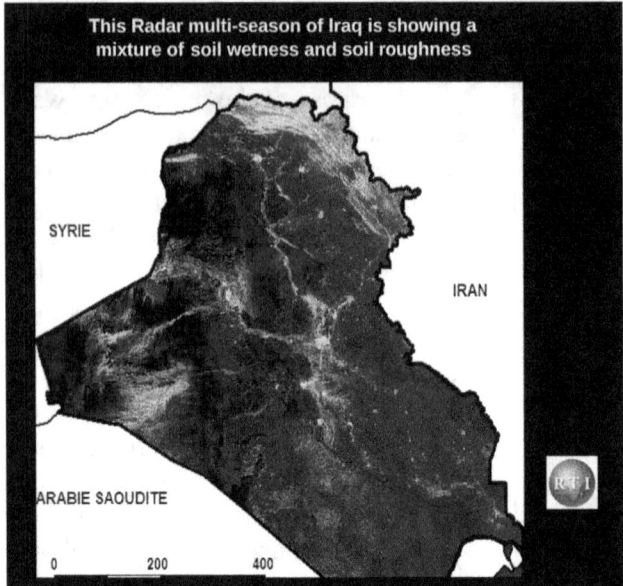

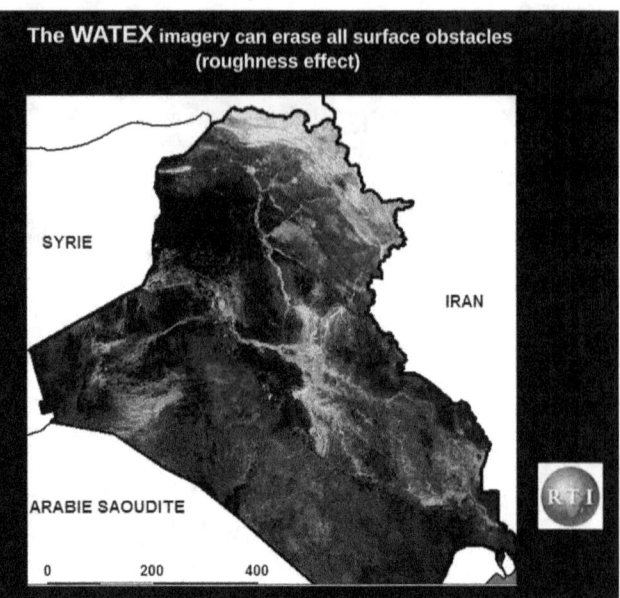

The comparison of a radar image (left) with WATEX technology (right) demonstrates that the new technology greatly improves the search for available groundwater.

results, promising this dry and extremely poor region hope for economic revival and survival. In 2015, Dr. Gachet and RTI completed the mapping of all the groundwater resources of Iraq in a project sponsored by UNESCO [**Figure 7**]. His results give great hope to the fight against desertification in Iraq, and support the Schiller Institute's findings of the importance of the Iraqi Green Belt. (A transcript of Dr. Gachet's presentation to the Schiller Institute Berlin Conference in June 2016 can be accessed at: http://www.larouchepub.com/ eiw/public/2016/eirv43n29-20160715/35-42_4329.pdf)

The usual criticism of focusing on groundwater as a long-term source of water for communities is that most of that water is fossil water that will be depleted and gone forever. WATEX and other modern theories of hydrology prove that the fossil water and completely "confined aquifers" is a myth. These new technologies prove that, while a great deal of water is stored for thousands of years in some underground aquifers such as the Grand Nubian Sandstone Aquifer, a great amount of water is continuously contributing to recharging aquifers through fracture systems deep underground and which extend to tens and sometimes hundreds of kilometers to other regions such as mountains with high rainfall. The only problem is that these systems have never been mapped. These new technologies can now finally tell us something about the 97% of all the fresh water of the planet which is under the surface.

Petrochemicals: Industry of the Future

The collapse of the global oil price since 2014, bringing down the price of a barrel to below $30 sometimes, rang alarm bells in the economies of all oil exporting countries. Most of these nations depend economically almost exclusively on the sales of oil and gas. This development posed serious questions regarding the future of the economies of Southwest Asia. The diversification of national income should be a self-evident matter. But there also should be focus on the areas of strength. For example, the countries of the region cannot become food exporters, because they suffer from prolonged periods of drought and water shortages. Although they have to endeavor to become more self-sufficient in food production, the strength of the economies of these nations lies in the abundance of hydrocarbon resources and the potential of moving from the role of raw oil exporters to industrial economies specialized in petrochemical production.

The global chemicals sector has long been dominated by the United States, Europe, and Japan. There are factors that say that this situation is changing and will have to change. Some oil industry officials in the region argue that the Middle East can offer an "energy advantage," i.e., an abundance of the fuel and feedstock that constitute the lifeblood of the petrochemical industry. In terms of fuel, the Middle East region boasts abundant supplies of competitively priced gas and liquids, meaning reduced costs for petrochemical facilities and lower costs of electric power generation. These low energy costs constitute a big competitive advantage, particularly in an energy-intensive business such as petrochemicals. For example, in the EU's chemical industry energy as a whole accounts for 10% to 60% of production costs for most products, meaning savings on energy expenditure can provide a big edge over higher cost competitors. Even more vital to the success of a petrochemical enterprise is the availability and cost of feedstock, whether gas- or liquids-based.

There is a common misconception in this argument, however, because in the near future nuclear power will—and should—replace gas as an energy source for the petrochemical industry. Natural gas will itself be used as a feedstock for chemicals and fertilizer industries. The other shortcoming in the strategic thinking of these countries' oil sector is that its development of massive petrochemical and refinery capacity has focused on producing and exporting "primary" or intermediary refined products with low added value, such as ethylene, propylene, butylene, and benzene. These primary products are used to generate greater added value somewhere else on the planet by producing a range of polymers (plastics), solvents, resins, fibers, detergents, ammonia, and other synthetic compounds.

Plastics properties make them ideal for a host of applications. Products made of plastic are stronger, lighter, more economical and recyclable. And ongoing improvements in the properties of polymers mean that plastics are more than ever a material of the future. The plastics are the single most crucial product in this sector. The most important application on a mass base is packaging, followed by building/construction. These two applications together consume almost 60% of the total Western-European plastic use. Plastics are used to make window frames, synthetic carpet, ducts and piping, room partitions, sound- and above all heat-insulation panels, and tanks to hold water, heating oil, and sewage. Plastics also have a role in electrical appliances, light fittings, furniture, toys, and electronics equipment. In electronics, they are a key component including in cell phones, TV sets, and computers. In the medical sector plastics go into every disposable item—syringes, blood pouches, heart valves, orthopedic apparatus, artificial limbs, medicine containers, and professional garments.

Even in the automotive sector plastics have started taking over an important share of components. Today's motor vehicles have fenders and spoilers made of plastic, and often some body panels, the fuel tank, and interior fittings such as dashboards and seats. About 20% of the parts under the hood are also plastic. Because plastics are lighter than metal, the vehicle is lighter too, and a weight saving can mean a significant reduction in motor-fuel consumption.

Another effect of developing the down-stream petrochemical industries is employment. Basic chemicals production offers little job opportunities, but there is substantial potential for job creation further down the product chain. Policy will have to be geared toward encouraging production of more sophisticated products as a means of creating more jobs for the country's young and rapidly expanding population.

A recent study by CEFIC, the European Chemical Industry Council, said that in the past 10 years, Europe's share of the world production of chemical products fell from 31% to around 27%, as Asia's rose from 13% to 23%. In 1990, the Middle East produced just under 3 million tons of ethylene, good for less than 5% of world production, compared with Europe's 30%. This rose to 12 million tons in 2005. With all the units that are soon to go on stream and all the gas fields in development, the projection is that the Middle East will soon overtake Europe. This rationale is not restricted to base products like ethylene and polymers, but also goes for finished products.

A contributing factor is that many European and American industries are moving to the region due to the cheap conventional energy source for the industry and the region's proximity to China and other emerging Asian economies that have become the world's largest consumers of petrochemicals.

One interesting aspect of the chemical and petrochemical industry is that it is closely connected to continuous scientific advancements and discoveries. As the German and French chemical industry historically gave birth to or created the environment for scientific breakthroughs in atomic science and space technologies, such as rocket science development, this sector can become the basis for creating a totally new science-oriented cultural paradigm, because it requires higher levels of education and skill.

As one study of the European chemical industry indicated: "Without the chemical industry, there is no chemistry, and without chemistry, there is no solution for the big challenges facing the world in the foreseeable future: 10 billion people with the resulting problems on energy, food and water supply."

Conference

2030 Mega Projects 2017

in the Egyptian Transport Sector for the "Ministry of Transport"

Connecting THE NEW ERA

Conference
11-12 October 2017

Cairo International Convention Center, CICC, Cairo, Egypt.

www.megaprojectsconf.com

Exhibitions
11-13 October 2017 | Cairo International Convention Center, CICC, Cairo, Egypt.

PHAROS
Exhibition 2017

International Exhibition for Transportation,
Maritime, Logistics, Ports & Shipping
"The Light of Opportunities"

www.pharos-event.com

Middle East Africa
Rail Show Exhibition 2017
Powered by **THE NEW SILKROAD**

International Exhibition for Railway Technologies,
Rail Systems, Mass Transport, Infrastructure,
Metro & Underground
"Development & Renovation"

Powered by
THE NEW SILK ROAD

www.marailshow.com

DON'T MISS OUR EARLY BIRD RATES .. REGISTER NOW !

South Africa Fights For Its Turn to the East

by David Cherry and Ramasimong Phillip Tsokolibane

April 8—The Empire struck back—with mass marches for regime-change on April 7—when South African President Jacob Zuma fired Finance Minister Pravin Gordhan, London's man, over March 30-31 in a major cabinet reshuffle. Zuma appointed in his place Malusi Gigaba, a partisan of the BRICS, who had been Home Affairs Minister. The fury of the City of London and Wall Street went off the charts, and reflected a difference of principle between the two ministers.

Pravin Gordhan had been fundamentally hostile to the vision of the BRICS, while doing his best not to appear so. Great projects? No, not today, thank you. He threw up obstacles against the very projects required to transform South Africa into a prosperous nation, one in which every family could look forward to a better life for its children. If you have wondered why the Johannesburg Regional Center of the New Development Bank (the BRICS bank)—which began hiring staff in March 2016—still does not have a director general, the answer lies in Gordhan's obstruction.

Malusi Gigaba presents a sharp contrast to Gordhan's imperial thinking. Last August 11, Gigaba, then Home Minister, attended the launch of the *BRICS Journal* in Johannesburg and was interviewed by Lameez Omarjee of the financial news website *Fin24* on the spot. Gigaba said that South Africa should:

industrialize, manufacture more, and trade more on manufactured goods, and the best platform for that is both the African continent as well as the BRICS countries and emerging countries in general. ...

We therefore need to view ourselves in relation to the continent and take a perspective that if the rest of the continent develops, infrastructure-wise, economically, politically, then South Africa's own role and position is further enhanced, and in so doing, in developing the African infrastructure story, we can use that very strongly to create your downstream industries, to create your supplier industries, to industrialize our economies on the basis of that infrastructure rollout, and ensure that through that, we can then be able to face up to other parts of the world. ...

Gigaba went on to attack the "hysteria" in the West about China and its role in Africa and elsewhere, according to which China is "out to gobble up our resources, to recolonize us." But, he said, we are no longer so weak, and we are more aware: "We have had an experience of centuries of colonialism." In this way, he drew out the laughable image of the perpetrators of ongoing imperialism in Africa being now so kind as to warn the continent against the alleged threat of imperialism from another quarter.

The New Development Bank, he said,

gives us the opportunity to leverage funding for our infrastructure investments in a way that must lead to industrialization, because in itself, infrastructure can be a driver for economic growth—and it will benefit from economic growth—and it can be a [word indistinct] for industrialization. That's what we need to use it for, and therefore, to take that leverage and engage with fellow BRICS countries in a manner that ensures that whatever investments they

Ex-Finance Minister Pravin Gordhan.

Government of South Africa

Finance Minister Malusi Gigaba.

make on the African continent, they are linked to industrialization, … [and] therefore build the stage of the African continent in the world.[1]

Gigaba's outlook rests on the same intentions that Nelson Mandela held and expressed upon being released from prison in 1990. And Mandela would have acted on those intentions if he had found a partner in U.S. President Bill Clinton. But beyond warmth and admiration, Clinton did nothing to enable Mandela to withstand the oligarchs of the British system, whom he did not have the courage to withstand, himself.

It was also President Mandela's decision, in 1996, to end South Africa's recognition of the Republic of China in favor of the People's Republic of China.

LaRouche Method in Action

LaRouche South Africa (LSA), led by one of us, Ramasimong Phillip Tsokolibane, has played a major role in inspiring the growing resistance to the tenacious imperial hand, the hand that captured the state more than 200 years ago, and has managed to keep it to this day. (Even National Party rule from 1948 to 1994, properly understood, was no exception.) The thrust of Tsokolibane's and LSA's method, learned from U.S. statesman Lyndon LaRouche—always situating major events and policy issues in terms of the higher, global strategic picture, and having confidence in the possibility of a better world—is evident in their record, summarized here:

Obama, mass murderer. LSA exposed President

---

1. See the embedded audio file in "Gigaba Challenges Western Media Perspectives on BRICS," http://www.fin24.com/Economy/gigaba-challenges-western-media-perspectives-on-brics-20160811

Obama as a mass murderer as he arrived to speak on the Soweto campus of the University of Johannesburg, June 29, 2013. Tsokolibane and LSA member Frank Sukwana were interviewed by a host of international press; the press featured their large posters of Obama with his Hitler moustache. Obama told his audience, in effect, that Africa would not be allowed to industrialize, since it would damage the planet.

Nuclear power and BRICS. On July 25, 2014 in *EIR*, Tsokolibane and his coauthor, David Cherry, celebrated President Zuma's decision to add 9,600 megawatts of nuclear power to South Africa's existing nuclear power production of 1,860 megawatts—in combination with his already established policy of vigorous participation in the BRICS.

Regime change. In the same *EIR* article, the authors first warned of regime change—months before the National Union of Metalworkers (NUMSA) and Rev. Barney Pityana first publicly called for regime change in December 2014. They warned: "The British financial empire will seek all possible avenues to disrupt the implementation of South Africa's nuclear plans and crush the assertion of sovereignty that made those plans possible. The empire has seen this moment coming. It has the been laying the groundwork for another of its regime change operations—as seen in Iraq, Libya, Georgia, Ukraine, and elsewhere."

Nuclear for all Africa. On July 21, 2014, LSA issued a statement demanding nuclear power for Africa, to include "many safe, South African-designed Pebble Bed reactors throughout the continent. To be truly free, we must have cheap, abundant energy, to power all other development, including the provision of fresh water." Conventional nuclear power and later fusion are the only path to that end, and "If Africa does not go nuclear, then it will die." At the annual Nuclear Africa conference in 2016, Tsokolibane and LSA member Samuel Lepele had opportunities to tell nuclear specialists and government officials about BRICS and the possibility of financing nuclear via the BRICS' New Development Bank. South Africa resumed its work on the Pebble Bed reactor in 2016.

Regime change networks. Tsokolibane and Cherry, in "No to British Regime Change in South Africa!" *EIR*, Jan. 16, 2015, exposed previously unrecognized regime change connections between figures such as Gene Sharp and Michael Burawoy in the United States, and their collaborators at the University of the Witwatersrand, the University of Johannesburg, and elsewhere.

EIRNS

Lyndon LaRouche stands next to Samuel Lepele of LaRouche South Africa, at the Sept. 15-16, 2007 Schiller Institute conference on the Eurasian Land-Bridge, in Kiedrich, Germany. From the right are the authors of this article: Ramasimong Phillip Tsokolibane of South Africa and David Cherry.

Mobilization for BRICS. LSA urgently called on government to educate and rally the people around the BRICS and its vision. Its statement, released Jan. 16, 2015, titled "Will You Allow the British Empire to Finally Destroy South Africa?" also stated, "Not enough of our citizens even know what the BRICS is, let alone that the BRICS policy represents the only hope." President Zuma and others in government, such as Malusi Gigaba, have since taken on this responsibility.

The BRICS vision. Tsokolibane spoke on "Developing Africa through the BRICS" on March 29, 2015 at the Melbourne, Australia conference of the Citizens Electoral Council titled, "The World Land Bridge: Peace on Earth, Goodwill Towards All Men."

'Maidan Square' threat. Tsokolibane published "Regime Change Movement, Against BRICS and Nuclear Power, Is 'Marching to Pretoria'" on the *News24* website on June 24, 2015, after the announcement of an Aug. 19 mega-march on Pretoria. He provided evidence that pre-arranged violence by provocateurs was likely. *Pretoria News* provided a link to the article. Within 24 hours, however, the article and its cached version came down for reasons unknown (but easily guessed—Patrick Gaspard was the U.S. ambassador). The article had hit its mark. The cacophony of the press against Zuma subsided temporarily, the march was

postponed, and *Citizen* editor Steven Motale published on Aug. 12 his powerful column, "I'm sorry, President Zuma," which begins, "I've been party to the sinister agenda against Zuma, and can only apologize."

New Suez Canal. Tsokolibane broke the blackout in the South African press of Egyptian President Abdel Fattah el-Sisi's impressive and just completed project to expand the capacity of the Suez Canal, in a column in *Pretoria News*, Aug. 21, 2015.

Letter to Trump. After President Trump declared that his administration would put an end to continual war and regime change operations, Tsokolibane wrote to him on March 16, 2017. His letter said, in part, "I ask that you authorize a thoroughgoing investigation of individuals and organizations, both inside the U.S. government and outside, especially those U.S.-based organizations associated with Mr George Soros, regarding their involvement in coup and 'regime change' activity against the elected government of President Jacob Zuma of South Africa. I also ask that you to order all U.S. government agencies and individuals, including those associated with the U.S. State Department, and including left-overs from the Obama Administration, to immediately cease all support for regime change activities directed against the government of South Africa."

U.S. regime change probe. When U.S. Senator Mike Lee announced that he and other senators were probing State Department regime change operations in Macedonia, Tsokolibane wrote to him on March 20, 2017, to propose that he extend his inquiry to include such operations in South Africa. He wrote, in part, that his associates affiliated with Lyndon LaRouche have provided leads that point to Obama and his State Department henchmen, including former U.S. Ambassador Mr. Patrick Gaspard, now the vice president of George Soros' Open Society Foundations, with responsibility for strategic direction and oversight of the agenda. Soros' operatives, Tsokolibane wrote, are at the center of the efforts to oust President Zuma and reverse his policy for South Africa to play a key role in the BRICS alliance.

This summary shows that method is right and the results are good, but the shutdown of the regime change networks has not yet been accomplished. That is evidenced by the April 7 demonstrations, even though they were weak. Demonstrations are but one strategic prong. There are other battle fronts, such as the upcoming attempt to get a vote of No Confidence in parliament, that will work in synergy with the demonstrations; there is still great danger.

The April 7 Demonstrations

Possibly as many as 50-60,000 people demonstrated "against Zuma" in all cities combined. About 15,000 of the total reportedly gathered in the largest demonstration, at Union Buildings, the seat of government in Pretoria. The government's nuanced security work was well planned and well executed, leaving little room for incidents to get out of hand.

The managers of the demonstrations were themselves not pleased with the puny size of these crowds. One commentator in the financial press used crowd sizes in the recent regime change in Brazil (as a percentage of total population) as a measure. The April 7 crowds in South Africa were largely middle class gatherings and did not draw all urban elements. Half of South Africa's urban population lives either in the impoverished townships or as squatters in "informal settlements," and this half of the urban population did not march. And, the leadership of the Congress of South African Trade Unions (COSATU)—in spite of having bought into the anti-Zuma propaganda—ordered its members not to participate.

COSATU came to understand that the unconstitutional removal of the President would be the real source of harm to South Africa's democracy which, by default, is in the custodianship of the ruling African National Congress (ANC). When former President Thabo Mbeki was unceremoniously removed from office in 2008, it had split the ANC, just as George Soros had wished for a few years ago, during a visit to Cape Town.

Who Runs 'Save South Africa'?

Regime change or "color revolution" is a way to win wars without having to fight them. *It is a form of war.* Its history in imperialist practice has been examined in earlier *EIR* articles.[2]

The April 7 demonstrations across South Africa were

Cape Town Guy

Anti-Zuma March in Cape Town, April 7.

largely under the aegis of "Save South Africa," which managed its operations through international big business, with the Oppenheimer family's Anglo American Corporation taking leadership. But it would be wrong to seek to understand such regime change operations as being ultimately controlled by and for big business. They are, rather, controlled by and for the oligarchs—the elite of the elites—and big business is a tool with extensive capabilities that is well aligned in outlook.

The "Save South Africa" operation—which has promised to deliver more and bigger demonstrations in the coming days and weeks—is led by the British-trained Sipho Pityana, chairman of the board of AngloGold Ashanti (17% owned by Anglo American), with input from George Soros' Open Society network, British agent Richard Calland, and others. In early September 2016, in forming Save South Africa, Pityana brought together a core of like-minded big-money people in business; the academics, political opposition leaders, and NGOs were brought in later.

Pityana is not well qualified as a righteous critic of the wrongdoing of others. He joined the board of AngloGold Ashanti—one of the world's biggest gold mining companies—in February 2007 when it was 42% owned by Anglo American. In August 2008, War on Want, the British NGO, published "Anglo American: The Alternative Report," in which it said of AngloGold,

Trade unionists who have stood up against AngloGold Ashanti mining operations in Colombia have been murdered by military units assigned to protect the company, while the company's links

2. Such as David Cherry and Ramasimong Phillip Tsokolibane, "No to British Regime Change in South Africa!": http://www.larouchepub.com/eiw/public/2015/eirv42n03-20150116/44-55_4203.pdf and Rachel Douglas, "Destabilizing Russia: The 'Democracy' Agenda of McFaul and His Oxford Masters": http://www.larouchepub.com/other/2012/3905destab_russia_mcfaul.html

with armed groups responsible for human rights abuses in the DRC have raised serious questions over its continuing presence there.

In January 2011, AngloGold was named the world's "Most Irresponsible Company" at the Public Eye Awards in Davos, Switzerland, and was accused there of a history of "gross human rights violations and environmental problems." *GhanaWeb*'s news report on the event is titled, "Anglo-Gold Is World's Most Evil Company."

Sipho Pityana, leader of the "Save South Africa" operation seeking to implement regime change in South Africa.

AngloGold Ashanti—of which Pityana has been chairman of the board since 2013—attempted to clean itself up by initiating a conference to jawbone about "Ecumenical Reflections on Mining," held at the Archbishop of Canterbury's Lambeth Palace in October 2014.

This Pityana is the chief of the self-righteous coup organizers against democratically elected President Zuma. Pityana's combined salary and bonus from AngloGold alone was $411,250 as reported in 2016, not to mention his income from other directorships and chairmanships, such his chairmanship of Munich Reinsurance of Africa.

His brother, Rev. Barney Pityana, rector of the Anglican College in South Africa and Fellow of King's College London, was one of the first to openly promote regime change in South Africa, long before Save South Africa was formed. He stood the truth on its head when he told a meeting in Johannesburg, convened by Democracy Works on Dec. 4, 2014, "Indeed we do want regime change, because that is what democracy is all about."

The organizer of Save South Africa's Pretoria rally on April 7 was Mark Heywood, one of those numerous fake Marxists who learned to play the part at Oxford University. Heywood's college at Oxford was Balliol, famous as a nursery for intelligence operatives. In Port Elizabeth, the Save South Africa rally was organized by a close associate of Sipho

Oxford-trained Mark Heywood organized Save South Africa's Pretoria rally on April 7.

Pityana, Mkhuseli Jack, a wealthy Eastern Cape businessman who funded the Congress of the People (COPE) party when it split off from the ruling ANC in 2008.

The 'Logic' of Regime Change

The architects of the regime change operation, with the help of the mainstream media, are indoctrinating South Africans with two absurd mantras: First, that "Zuma is the problem, and if we can overthrow him, and get rid of his friends, the Gupta brothers, then corruption will be gone and all will be well." So, then, South Africans will be guided by fine fellows such as Sipho Pityana. Second, that "Zuma is a dictator, and because he violates the constitution, we must throw him out by unconstitutional means to save the constitution." South Africa's constitutional system may be weaker than desired, but Zuma was elected in a fair contest, and appears to retain majority support. *The real purpose of regime change is ungovernability.* That should be obvious, especially for the "educated" people who seem now to accept what they are being told, that their moral self-righteousness and group-think trump all.

Bertrand Russell wrote, "In order to condition students, verses set to music and repeatedly intoned are very effective. . . . It is for a future scientist ... to discover exactly how much it costs per head to make children believe that snow is black."

It is the same kind of operation that is being run in the United States against President Trump. His enemies—the same oligarchical enemies that Zuma faces—fear that Trump just might carry out some of the policies that he initially announced: an end to confrontation with Russia and China, an end to endless wars, an end to regime change operations, and a return to the American System of economy instead of the prevailing "loot thy neighbor" policy.

dacherry3@yahoo.com
ramasimongt@hotmail.com

www.ingramcontent.com/pod-product-compliance
Lightning Source LLC
Chambersburg PA
CBHW081604280526
45788CB00011B/3553